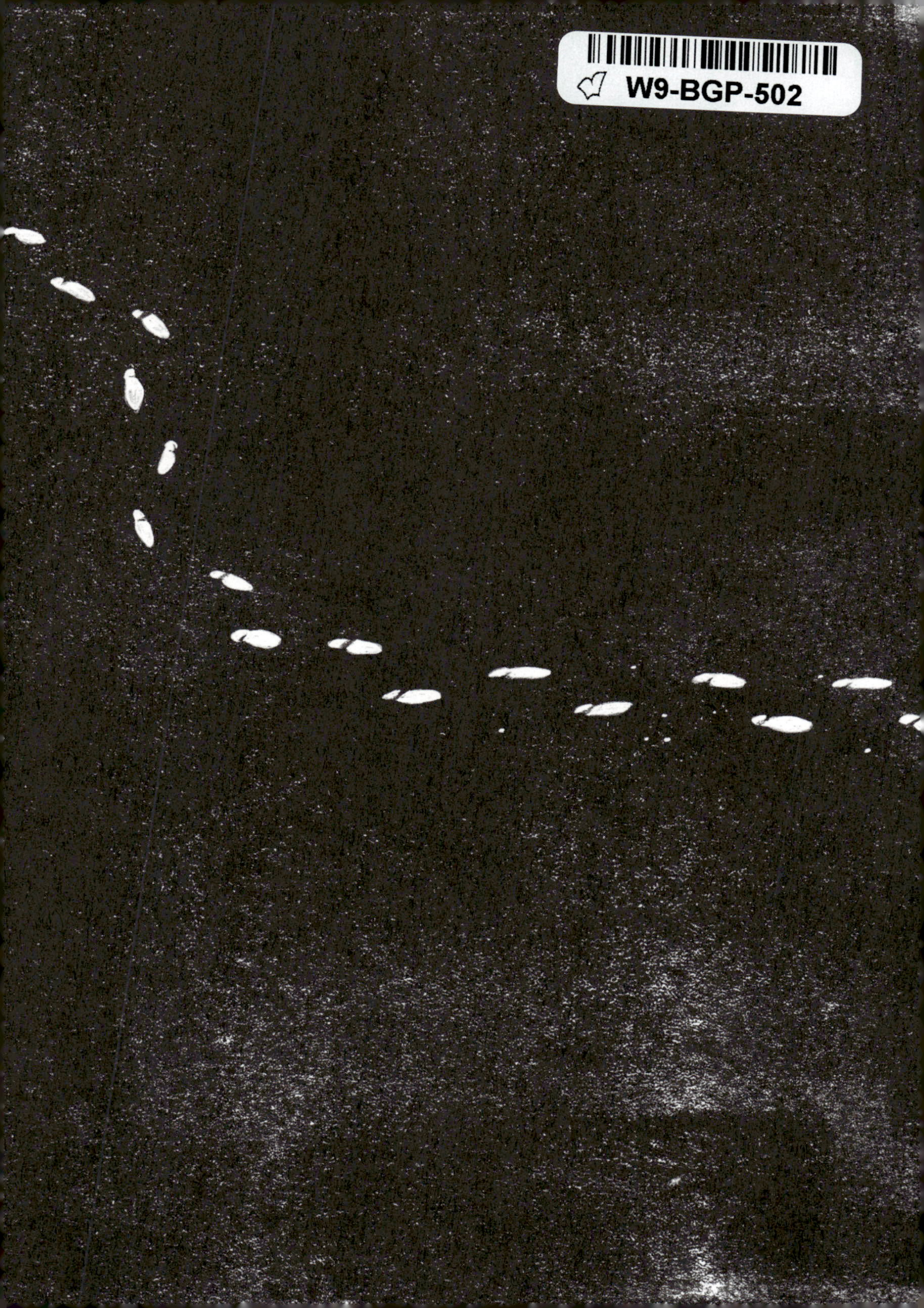

DIETRICH FELT THE TWIGS SNAP
beneath his bare heels as
they punched through the
unusual April frost.

The Lord walked next to him.
He had always been there, but
now Dietrich could almost see him,
as if just on the other side of a veil.

He knelt and prayed aloud
for a final time.
Dietrich closed his eyes.

The Lord drew near.
Ever closer.
Ever closer.

"This is the end—

"...for me THE BEGINNING OF LIFE.*"

—DIETRICH BONHOEFFER'S FINAL RECORDED WORDS

DIETRICH BONHOEFFER AND THE PLOT TO KILL HITLER

THE FAITHFUL SPY

JOHN HENDRIX

AMULET BOOKS, NEW YORK

This book follows the life of the man DIETRICH BONHOEFFER. But it is equally a story of the German resistance. It is a story that often goes untold.

When Adolf Hitler, a homicidal tyrant unmatched in modern history, came to power, he began a campaign of destruction. He gleefully led the world into its second war in twenty years. By the end, Hitler's shameful résumé included the extermination of millions of Jews and ethnic minorities, the slaughter of legions of his own men on foolish military strategies, and the obliteration of the civilian landscape of Europe. But—sometimes overlooked—he also stole the soul of Germany.

Hitler had surrounded himself with henchmen and cronies who were more demons than dignitaries. Hitler and these ministers of evil carried the legacy of a proud and kind people with them into hell. To be sure, the nation's people bear a heavy responsibility, but we are wrong to see the German citizens as made of only one fabric. Although it is no balm for the victims of the Nazi horrors, we should be careful before we condemn all of Germany along with Hitler's devils.

Desperate for leadership, the German people were led like rats to the edge of the cliff by a diabolical Pied Piper. But not all fell for the seduction. Dietrich was but one man among many hundreds of patriotic Germans (including prominent preachers, military generals, and politicians) who saw the Nazis for what they truly were and fought back. They fought with words at first, but eventually, they fought with actions.

These brave men and women risked all to "jam the spoke" of the Nazi war machine. Ultimately, they were unsuccessful. The forces opposing the German resistance were too massive to overcome. Hitler's legion of destruction would not be stopped before it had ground the glorious old Germany and its people into a hideous pulp. Hitler's end came only after total war, and his sins were visited upon the entire world.

Dietrich Bonhoeffer was one of the first in Europe to detect and decry the foul aroma of death surrounding Hitler in his treatment of the Jewish people. Through his devout faith in God, Bonhoeffer saw this hatred for what it was and began to sound the alarm as the hurricane gathered on the horizon.

SADLY, HIS BELOVED GERMANY FAILED TO LISTEN.

CHAPTER 1
THE YOUNG THEOLOGIAN

THIS IS DIETRICH.
OUR STORY BEGINS
AND ENDS WITH HIM.

AT EIGHTEEN, DIETRICH WAS ALREADY TRAINING TO BE A THEOLOGIAN

in Berlin, Germany. He enjoyed studying how humanity thinks about God—in his case, the God of the Bible. Dietrich Bonhoeffer had always loved thinking about God.

When Dietrich was a child, he and his twin sister, Sabine, would lie awake at night and try to comprehend the idea of eternity. What would it feel like to live forever? Staring up at the ceiling as they tried to fall asleep, the two would just say the word "eternity" over and over, trying to conjure a never-ending vision of heaven itself. In German, "eternity" is the word "Ewigkeit."

EWIGKEIT.
EWIGKEIT.
EWIGKEIT!

HIS MOTHER REMEMBERED HOW,
WHEN HE WAS ONLY FOUR,
DIETRICH'S MIND ALREADY LOVED THEOLOGICAL QUESTIONS.

DOES THE GOOD GOD LOVE THE CHIMNEY SWEEP TOO?

DOES GOD, TOO, SIT DOWN TO LUNCH?*

DIETRICH— AGE 4

*TEXTS MARKED WITH AN ASTERISK DENOTE DIRECT QUOTATIONS FROM OTHER SOURCES. DIALOGUE OR SPOKEN WORDS WITHOUT AN ASTERISK SHOULD BE READ AS SPECULATIVE.

Dietrich Bonhoeffer

The Bonhoeffer family loved music and sang hymns and carols together throughout the year. Dietrich himself was something of a virtuoso piano player and had considered a career in music before theology grabbed his heart.

BORN: 2/6/1906

BORN IN BRESLAU, GERMANY (NOW WROCLAW, POLAND)

NOT WEARING GLASSES YET

SHEET MUSIC HE WROTE

ALWAYS WORE NICE CLOTHES

DIETRICH LIVED IN A COUNTRY AT THE HEIGHT OF ITS POWER, CULTURAL INFLUENCE, AND SOPHISTICATED LUXURIES. HIS FAMILY WAS FORTUNATE TO BE WELL EDUCATED AND CULTURED IN ART, SCIENCE, AND MUSIC.

EXCELLENT PIANO PLAYER

STOCKY ATHLETIC FRAME
LOVED PLAYING GAMES

VERY GOOD SINGER

TABLE TENNIS WAS A FAVORITE.

Dietrich and his family belonged to the Lutheran church, a Protestant branch of Christianity. For as long as he could remember, Dietrich's family had read stories from the Bible together before they went to bed. Dietrich adored these supernatural tales filled with heroes, prophets, and kings. When he knelt down to pray, he felt connected to a world beyond himself, a cosmos greater than anything around him. It was as if the Lord were right beside him. He longed to be a man of God, full of faith and courage, like young King David. As a boy armed with a rock and a sling, David stood against the mighty warrior Goliath and slew him in a single blow.

Dietrich grew up in a big and wonderful family. His parents were demanding and asked for only the very best from their children, but the home vibrated with life and love. The Bonhoeffers' house in Berlin was as big as his family. Dietrich was one of eight brothers and sisters, including his twin, Sabine, and they and their parents, plus several caretakers would be in the house on a typical day.

BONHOEFFER FAMILY TREE

DIETRICH'S FATHER WAS A VERY WELL-KNOWN AND FAMOUS PSYCHOLOGIST AND NEUROLOGIST.

KARL WAS AN AUSTERE MAN BUT TOOK GREAT JOY IN HIS CHILDREN'S INTELLECTUAL LIFE. HE WOULD OFTEN REQUIRE THE CHILDREN TO PRESENT IDEAS WITH FORMAL ARGUMENTS FOR DISCUSSION AT DINNERTIME.

PAULA'S TEMPERAMENT WAS QUITE DIFFERENT FROM HER HUSBAND'S. SHE WAS A CARING AND TENDER MOTHER WHO LOVED PLANNING ELABORATE COSTUME PARTIES FOR FRIENDS AND HER CHILDREN. A WOMAN OF DEEP FAITH, SHE ALSO SHARED KARL'S DEVOTION TO SCIENCE AND KNOWLEDGE.

KARL BONHOEFFER
B. 1868

PAULA BONHOEFFER
B. 1874

8 KIDS

1 **KARL-FRIEDRICH**
B. 1899

2 **WALTER**
B. 1899

3 **KLAUS**
B. 1901

4 **URSULA**
B. 1902

5 **CHRISTINE**
B. 1903

TWINS

6 **SABINE**
B. 1906

7 **DIETRICH**
B. 1906

KARL-FRIEDRICH WAS LIKE HIS NAMESAKE FATHER IN EVERY WAY, AND HE LOVED CHEMISTRY AND SCIENCE.

8 **SUSANNE**
B. 1906

In 1920, at the age of fourteen, Dietrich declared he was a theologian! Dietrich's brothers and sisters were all very intelligent. His older brothers loved studying math and science. So young Dietrich was a bit of an odd duck in a family of future lawyers and scientists. They didn't understand why Dietrich was so interested in God and often teased him by calling him, quite formally, "My Brother: the Theologian!"

D, WHY MUST YOU CONCERN YOURSELF WITH, OF ALL THINGS, THE CHURCH?

WITHOUT THE CHURCH, WHAT ELSE IS THERE?

I CAN'T THINK OF A MORE FEEBLE, BORING, PETTY, AND IRRELEVANT INSTITUTION!

. . .

IN THAT CASE, I SHALL REFORM IT!*

DIETRICH

KLAUS, DIETRICH'S BROTHER

Even Dietrich's father, Karl, who was a kind but very pragmatic man, thought his interest in the church at such a young age was strange. But nothing could deter young Dietrich from learning all he could about the art and science of faith. He only wanted to be known as a real theologian. But, Dietrich's childhood wasn't perfect. The tragic events that would lead him towards a life of studying God had begun a few years earlier in 1914.

THE GREAT WAR HAD COME.

Today, we call the Great War World War I because of the second great war that would come after it.

The war effort came into the Bonhoeffer home when Dietrich's older brothers Karl-Friedrich and Walter were called up into military service in the German infantry. Early in the war, there was nationwide elation (near glee!) for the prospect of a grand adventure on the battlefield. The country was possessed with a patriotic desire to prove its mettle. But the terrible losses of life began to mount, and after four years of misery, the national mood had permanently soured. Victory, which had once seemed inevitable, was now a murky concept.

In April 1918, a messenger of the German government knocked on the Bonhoeffers' door. Walter had been killed on the western front. An exploding shell had gravely injured him. He had survived only long enough for a lingering infection to finish the job. Dietrich's world changed that day. As he prayed that night, he felt angry. He wondered why God had taken Walter from his family.

Where was his Lord in this suffering?
Why had God not protected Walter?

DIETRICH'S CHILDHOOD WAS OVER.

IN FACT, THE IDYLLIC GERMANY
DIETRICH HAD KNOWN AS A CHILD WAS ITSELF
COMING TO AN END. THE DECADES OF STABILITY AND PROSPERITY
UNDER THE EMPEROR OF GERMANY (CALLED THE KAISER) HAD CRUMBLED
WITH THE GROWING SENSE THAT THE UNTHINKABLE WOULD HAPPEN:

COULD MIGHTY GERMANY LOSE THE WAR?

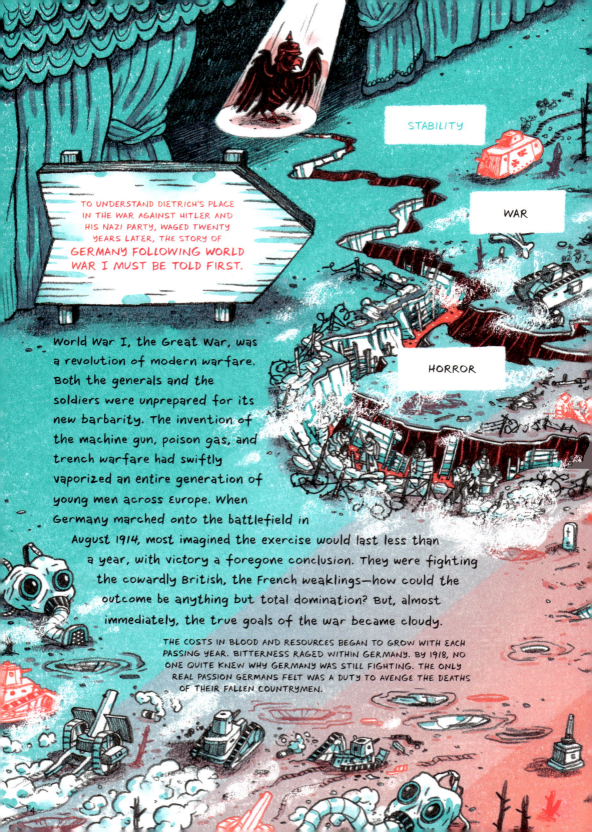

STABILITY

WAR

HORROR

TO UNDERSTAND DIETRICH'S PLACE IN THE WAR AGAINST HITLER AND HIS NAZI PARTY, WAGED TWENTY YEARS LATER, THE STORY OF **GERMANY FOLLOWING WORLD WAR I MUST BE TOLD FIRST.**

World War I, the Great War, was a revolution of modern warfare. Both the generals and the soldiers were unprepared for its new barbarity. The invention of the machine gun, poison gas, and trench warfare had swiftly vaporized an entire generation of young men across Europe. When Germany marched onto the battlefield in August 1914, most imagined the exercise would last less than a year, with victory a foregone conclusion. They were fighting the cowardly British, the French weaklings—how could the outcome be anything but total domination? But, almost immediately, the true goals of the war became cloudy.

THE COSTS IN BLOOD AND RESOURCES BEGAN TO GROW WITH EACH PASSING YEAR. BITTERNESS RAGED WITHIN GERMANY. BY 1918, NO ONE QUITE KNEW WHY GERMANY WAS STILL FIGHTING. THE ONLY REAL PASSION GERMANS FELT WAS A DUTY TO AVENGE THE DEATHS OF THEIR FALLEN COUNTRYMEN.

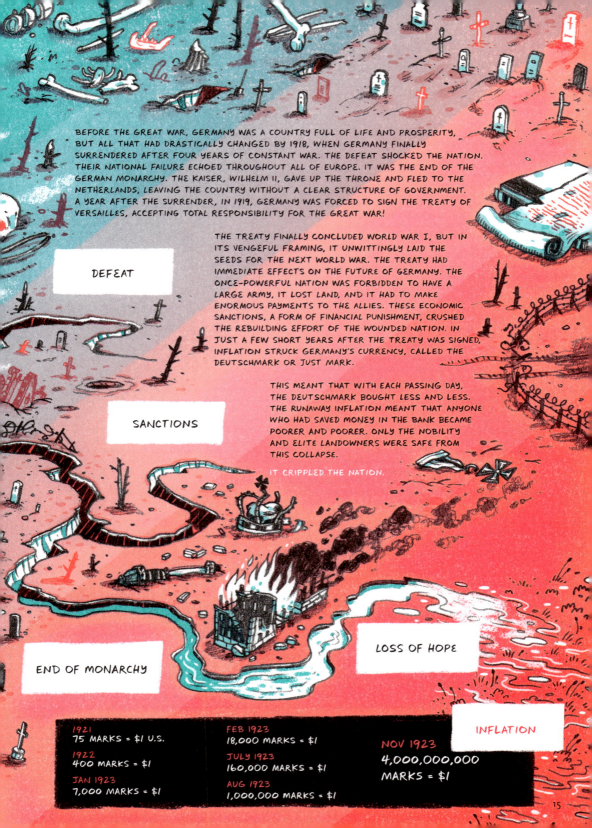

BEFORE THE GREAT WAR, GERMANY WAS A COUNTRY FULL OF LIFE AND PROSPERITY, BUT ALL THAT HAD DRASTICALLY CHANGED BY 1918, WHEN GERMANY FINALLY SURRENDERED AFTER FOUR YEARS OF CONSTANT WAR. THE DEFEAT SHOCKED THE NATION. THEIR NATIONAL FAILURE ECHOED THROUGHOUT ALL OF EUROPE. IT WAS THE END OF THE GERMAN MONARCHY. THE KAISER, WILHELM II, GAVE UP THE THRONE AND FLED TO THE NETHERLANDS, LEAVING THE COUNTRY WITHOUT A CLEAR STRUCTURE OF GOVERNMENT. A YEAR AFTER THE SURRENDER, IN 1919, GERMANY WAS FORCED TO SIGN THE TREATY OF VERSAILLES, ACCEPTING TOTAL RESPONSIBILITY FOR THE GREAT WAR!

THE TREATY FINALLY CONCLUDED WORLD WAR I, BUT IN ITS VENGEFUL FRAMING, IT UNWITTINGLY LAID THE SEEDS FOR THE NEXT WORLD WAR. THE TREATY HAD IMMEDIATE EFFECTS ON THE FUTURE OF GERMANY. THE ONCE-POWERFUL NATION WAS FORBIDDEN TO HAVE A LARGE ARMY, IT LOST LAND, AND IT HAD TO MAKE ENORMOUS PAYMENTS TO THE ALLIES. THESE ECONOMIC SANCTIONS, A FORM OF FINANCIAL PUNISHMENT, CRUSHED THE REBUILDING EFFORT OF THE WOUNDED NATION. IN JUST A FEW SHORT YEARS AFTER THE TREATY WAS SIGNED, INFLATION STRUCK GERMANY'S CURRENCY, CALLED THE DEUTSCHMARK OR JUST MARK.

DEFEAT

THIS MEANT THAT WITH EACH PASSING DAY, THE DEUTSCHMARK BOUGHT LESS AND LESS. THE RUNAWAY INFLATION MEANT THAT ANYONE WHO HAD SAVED MONEY IN THE BANK BECAME POORER AND POORER. ONLY THE NOBILITY AND ELITE LANDOWNERS WERE SAFE FROM THIS COLLAPSE.

SANCTIONS

IT CRIPPLED THE NATION.

END OF MONARCHY

LOSS OF HOPE

INFLATION

1921 75 MARKS = $1 U.S.	FEB 1923 18,000 MARKS = $1	NOV 1923
1922 400 MARKS = $1	JULY 1923 160,000 MARKS = $1	4,000,000,000 MARKS = $1
JAN 1923 7,000 MARKS = $1	AUG 1923 1,000,000 MARKS = $1	

MILLIONS OF PEOPLE IN GERMANY WERE OUT OF WORK. THEY WERE POOR, HUNGRY, AND ASHAMED OF BEING A DEFEATED PEOPLE.

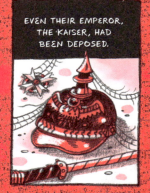

EVEN THEIR EMPEROR, THE KAISER, HAD BEEN DEPOSED.

AFTER THE MONARCHY ENDED IN 1918, THE GERMAN PEOPLE NO LONGER HAD ANY FORM OF GOVERNMENT THEY TRUSTED OR BELIEVED IN.

THE AFTERMATH OF WORLD WAR I IN THE HOMELAND OF GERMANY WAS NOTHING SHORT OF A TOTAL BANKRUPTCY OF THEIR CULTURAL HISTORY.

THEY WANTED TO FIND SOME KIND OF HOPE FOR THE FUTURE. WHO WOULD SAVE THEM?

THIS VACUUM OF CONFIDENCE IN THEMSELVES AND THEIR GOVERNMENT MADE ROOM FOR SOME VERY EXTREME IDEAS. THERE WAS A YOUNG MAN, HIMSELF A VETERAN OF THE GREAT WAR, WHO WAS READY TO GRAB THE REINS OF POWER WHILE THE GREAT GERMAN HORSE WAS WITHOUT A RIDER.

HIS NAME WAS ADOLF HITLER.

DURING THE 1920S,

THE COUNTRY SLID FURTHER AND FURTHER ADRIFT. AS THE GERMAN LEADERSHIP TRIED TO FORM A GOVERNMENT THAT WOULD BRING STABILITY TO THE COUNTRY, ADOLF HITLER TRIED TO SEIZE THE GOVERNMENT FOR HIMSELF THROUGH FEAR AND INTIMIDATION. HITLER WAS THE NEW LEADER OF A BREAKAWAY GROUP OF ACTIVISTS CALLED THE NATIONAL SOCIALIST WORKERS' PARTY (LATER SHORTENED INTO THE WORD "NAZI"). THESE MEN WERE VERY ANGRY WITH THE CURRENT GERMAN GOVERNMENT, COMPOSED OF THE SAME DIPLOMATS WHO HAD AGREED TO SIGN THE HUMILIATING TREATY OF VERSAILLES.

THE NAZIS STIRRED UP POPULAR SUPPORT FOR AN UPRISING AGAINST THE GOVERNMENT LEADERS. HITLER GAVE FIERY SPEECHES OF HATRED AGAINST THE GERMAN AUTHORITIES WHO HAD "STABBED GERMANY IN THE BACK." DURING THIS TIME A SPECIAL GROUP OF PERSONAL ENFORCERS CALLED "THE SA" OR "STORM TROOPERS" FORMED AROUND HITLER TO PROTECT HIS NAZI MOVEMENT AND RALLIES.

THESE MEN WOULD BECOME VERY IMPORTANT GUARDIANS OF HITLER'S GROWING POWER IN THE COMING YEARS.

November 1923

Hitler and his proxy army of storm troopers attempted to grab control of the government through brute force—a coup or, in German, a "Putsch."

THE ATTEMPTED HIJACKING WAS ILL CONCEIVED AND QUICKLY THWARTED. HITLER, AS THE LEADER, WAS SWIFTLY ARRESTED FOR INSURRECTION. BUT HE SOMEHOW TURNED THIS DEFEAT INTO A TRIUMPH. HIS 1924 TRIAL BECAME A SENSATION, GALVANIZING POPULAR SUPPORT FOR HIS CAUSE.

WHILE INCARCERATED, HE WROTE A BOOK ABOUT HIS LIFE AND RADICAL IDEAS CALLED "MEIN KAMPF" ("MY STRUGGLE"), WHICH WAS PUBLISHED IN 1925.

THOUGH SENTENCED TO PRISON FOR TREASON, HITLER ONLY SERVED SIX MONTHS! HIS BOOK WAS HARDLY A BESTSELLER WHEN PUBLISHED, BUT IT LAID THE GROUNDWORK FOR WHAT WOULD BE HITLER'S LIFE PURSUIT:

A TOTAL GERMAN CONQUEST OF EUROPE AND THE ERADICATION OF THE JEWISH PEOPLE!

He wrote, "I had at last come to the conclusion that the Jew was no German."* Ever since his days in the trenches during the Great War, Hitler had been vocal about his distrust of the Jewish people. But he went beyond mere hatred. Hitler made a personal vow to destroy every Jew in the country. He believed that Germany would never rise again until the "poisoners are exterminated."* Playing on the nation's Christianity, Hitler didn't frame this struggle as political ... but spiritual! "The personification of the Devil as the symbol of all evil assumes the living shape of the Jew."*

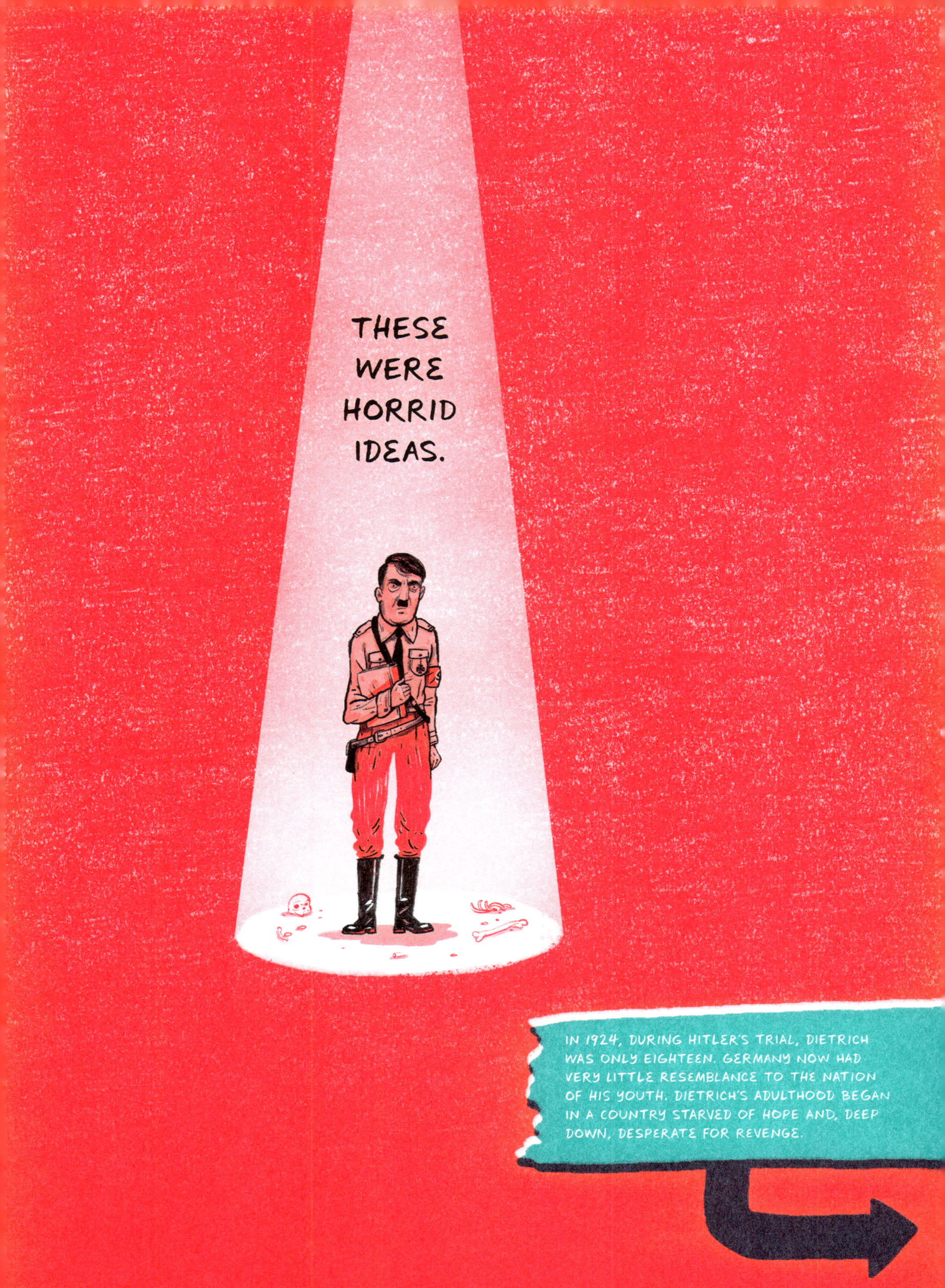
THESE WERE HORRID IDEAS.
IN 1924, DURING HITLER'S TRIAL, DIETRICH WAS ONLY EIGHTEEN. GERMANY NOW HAD VERY LITTLE RESEMBLANCE TO THE NATION OF HIS YOUTH. DIETRICH'S ADULTHOOD BEGAN IN A COUNTRY STARVED OF HOPE AND, DEEP DOWN, DESPERATE FOR REVENGE.

Despite the state of his broken nation, Dietrich studied at the University of Tübingen and the University of Berlin. Unlike some of his countrymen, he worked like a man with a proud and definite future. His all-consuming study of theology and philosophy was quite passionate, but he found it was not always personal. Dietrich felt like he studied God as if He were an animal in a zoo, making careful observations and measurements but always at a safe and comfortable distance.

WAS HE MERELY BECOMING GOD'S ZOOKEEPER?

Growing up in the Bonhoeffer household, he had been trained by his family to have a logical mind about everything.

But the more he studied God, the more his heart longed for something greater than knowledge. He was learning everything imaginable about the spiritual realms but felt increasingly alone.

He remembered the feeling he'd gotten from those Bible stories of his childhood— the heroes and saints who faced great danger, never clinging to their own efforts but to God alone! How he desired to feel that kind of certainty in his life.

DIETRICH'S THINKING CHANGED TRAJECTORY IN 1925.

THE YOUNG THEOLOGIAN WAS HUNGRY TO EXPERIENCE THE GRANDEUR OF GOD AND HIS CHURCH, SO HE MADE A PILGRIMAGE TO ROME, THE HOME OF CATHOLICISM. EVEN THOUGH DIETRICH WAS A LUTHERAN, HE HAD GREAT CURIOSITY ABOUT THE CATHOLIC CHURCH. HE VISITED THE SISTINE CHAPEL AND A DOZEN OTHER SITES AROUND ROME. BUT AS DIETRICH WATCHED THE CROWDS GATHER AT ST. PETER'S ON PALM SUNDAY, HE WAS STRUCK WITH THE SINGLE QUESTION:

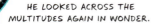

WHAT, EXACTLY, IS THE CHURCH?

SEEING THE THOUSANDS OF PEOPLE CELEBRATE TOGETHER ...

... LIBERATED DIETRICH FROM THE IDEA OF GOD AS JUST AN ACADEMIC EXERCISE.

HE LOOKED ACROSS THE MULTITUDES AGAIN IN WONDER.

DURING MASS, A BOYS' CHOIR SANG A HAUNTING INVOCATION THAT ROSE TO THE SKY IN GLORIOUS UNITY.

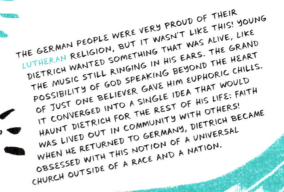

THE GERMAN PEOPLE WERE VERY PROUD OF THEIR LUTHERAN RELIGION, BUT IT WASN'T LIKE THIS! YOUNG DIETRICH WANTED SOMETHING THAT WAS ALIVE, LIKE THE MUSIC STILL RINGING IN HIS EARS. THE GRAND POSSIBILITY OF GOD SPEAKING BEYOND THE HEART OF JUST ONE BELIEVER GAVE HIM EUPHORIC CHILLS. IT CONVERGED INTO A SINGLE IDEA THAT WOULD HAUNT DIETRICH FOR THE REST OF HIS LIFE: FAITH WAS LIVED OUT IN COMMUNITY WITH OTHERS! WHEN HE RETURNED TO GERMANY, DIETRICH BECAME OBSESSED WITH THIS NOTION OF A UNIVERSAL CHURCH OUTSIDE OF A RACE AND A NATION.

"what could this universal church do if it left the comfort of the **SANCTUARY?**"

GERMANY WAS INESCAPABLY LUTHERAN IN BOTH HISTORY AND CULTURAL IDENTITY. LUTHERANISM, A DENOMINATION OF THE CHRISTIAN FAITH, WAS FOUNDED BY MARTIN LUTHER IN GERMANY IN 1517. LUTHER'S BREAKAWAY FROM THE CATHOLIC CHURCH WAS THE BEGINNING OF THE PROTESTANT CHURCH, CALLED THE REFORMATION.

Dietrich continued to study theology, but it no longer was merely academic. It was alive with possibility! He even wrote his doctoral dissertation in 1927 on this revelation, called "Sanctorum communio," or the communion of saints, asking what the church could do if God's people acted in the world with one voice. He concluded that the true church of God would not always agree with the world it inhabited, and so it must be revolutionary!

WOULD THE CHURCH, INDEED, ACT TOGETHER IN THE FACE OF INJUSTICE?

Meanwhile, Dietrich's countrymen were not experiencing the same joyful revelations as the young theologian.

In the years from 1925 to 1928, Hitler's party of nationalistic radicals continued to simmer just under the surface of German society. Though Hitler was banned from public speaking until 1927, he routinely ignored the law to rally his cadre of growing supporters. Many elite Germans saw him as merely an annoying fad. They agreed his views were barbaric and dismissed the potential of his lasting appeal.

NSDAP = NATIONAL SOCIALIST GERMAN WORKERS' PARTY, THE OFFICIAL NAME OF THE NAZIS. THE HAKENKREUZ OR SWASTIKA (HOOKED CROSS) WAS THE SYMBOL OF THE NAZI PARTY.

THE REICHSTAG

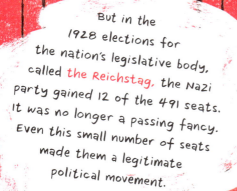

But in the 1928 elections for the nation's legislative body, called the Reichstag, the Nazi party gained 12 of the 491 seats. It was no longer a passing fancy. Even this small number of seats made them a legitimate political movement.

In October 1929, the world was devastated by the collapse of the global financial markets, which marked the beginning of the Great Depression. The event sent even the most stable countries, like the United States, into a tailspin. But for a country like Germany, still reeling from the financial terms of the Treaty of Versailles, it was a disaster.

HITLER WAS DELIGHTED. THIS CRACK IN GERMANY'S ECONOMIC FOUNDATION WAS JUST BIG ENOUGH TO LET HIS RATS INTO THE CELLAR.

CHAPTER 2
A YOUNG GERMAN IN HARLEM

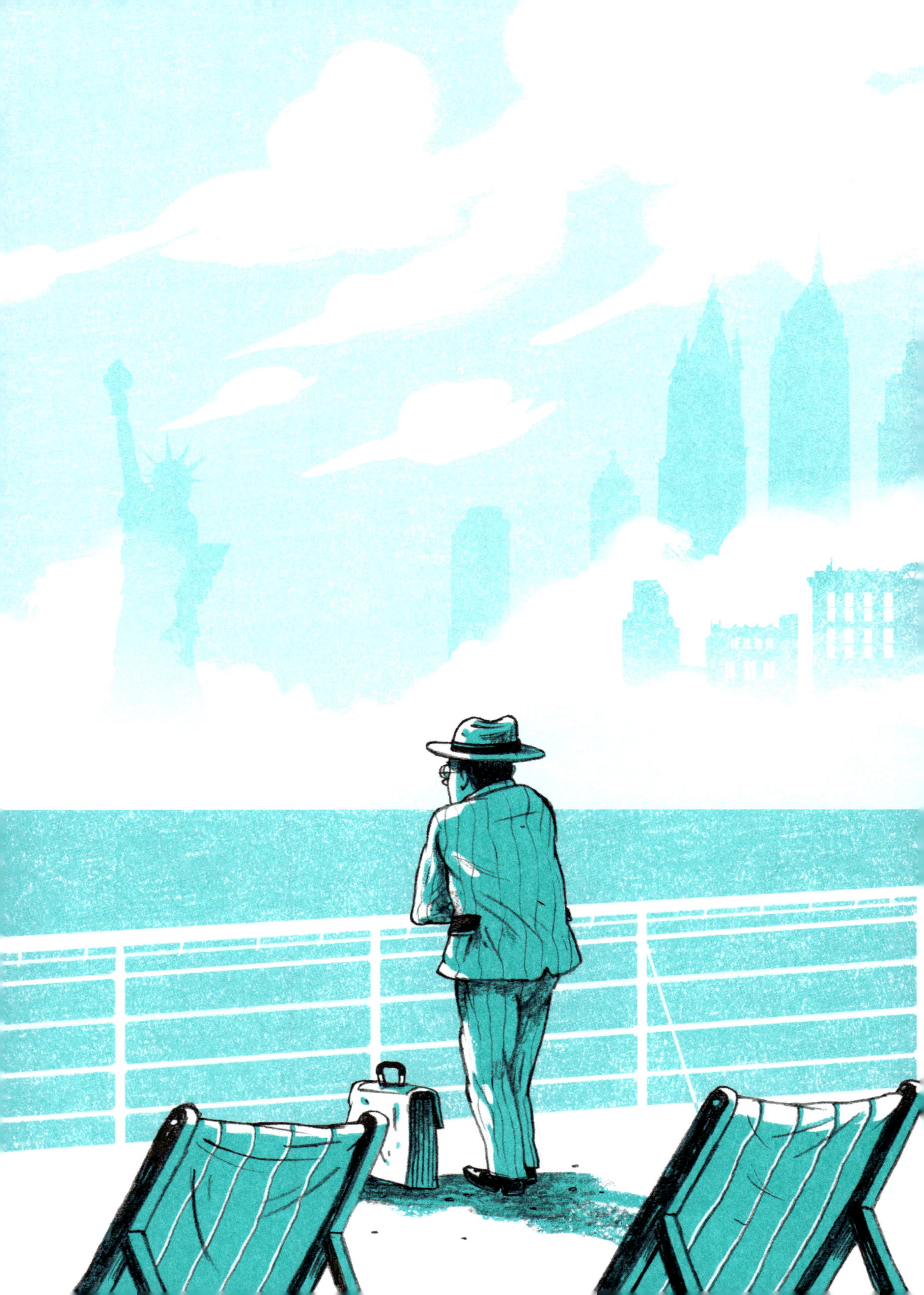

DIETRICH WAS IN NEW YORK CITY.

It was another vastly new experience. Although the stock market crash had happened the previous fall, the raw energy of the city hadn't been dampened yet. Everywhere he looked, there were glittering new buildings, record-breaking bridges, and silver-lined towers reaching to the sky.

He had come to the bustling city in 1930 to continue his studies at Union Theological Seminary, located just to the west of the neighborhood of Harlem. Dietrich loved to travel and, as during his time in Rome a few years earlier, he was eager to see how America would change his thinking. He was not disappointed. The year he spent in the United States changed the way he thought about people suffering oppression and systemic racism.

SIX YEARS HAVE PASSED SINCE DIETRICH VISITED ROME. HE WEARS GLASSES AND HAS LESS HAIR.

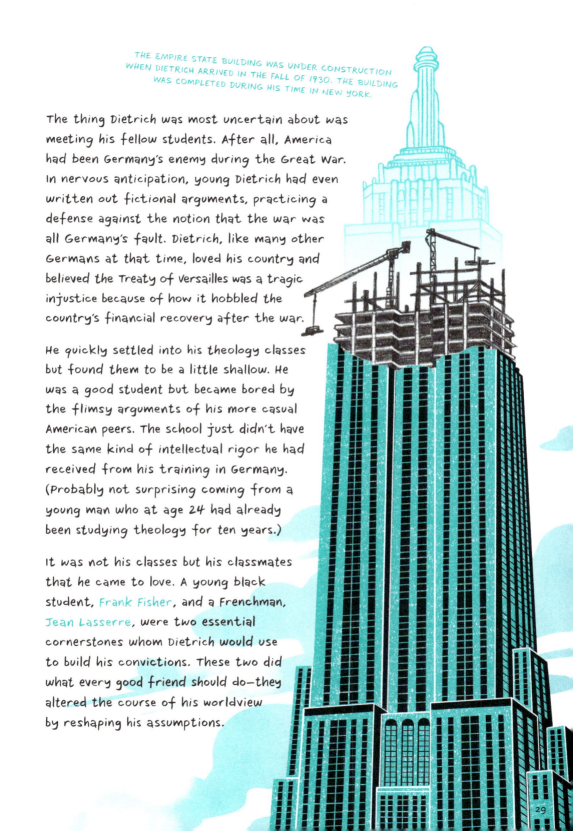

THE EMPIRE STATE BUILDING WAS UNDER CONSTRUCTION WHEN DIETRICH ARRIVED IN THE FALL OF 1930. THE BUILDING WAS COMPLETED DURING HIS TIME IN NEW YORK.

The thing Dietrich was most uncertain about was meeting his fellow students. After all, America had been Germany's enemy during the Great War. In nervous anticipation, young Dietrich had even written out fictional arguments, practicing a defense against the notion that the war was all Germany's fault. Dietrich, like many other Germans at that time, loved his country and believed the Treaty of Versailles was a tragic injustice because of how it hobbled the country's financial recovery after the war.

He quickly settled into his theology classes but found them to be a little shallow. He was a good student but became bored by the flimsy arguments of his more casual American peers. The school just didn't have the same kind of intellectual rigor he had received from his training in Germany. (Probably not surprising coming from a young man who at age 24 had already been studying theology for ten years.)

It was not his classes but his classmates that he came to love. A young black student, Frank Fisher, and a Frenchman, Jean Lasserre, were two essential cornerstones whom Dietrich would use to build his convictions. These two did what every good friend should do—they altered the course of his worldview by reshaping his assumptions.

FRANK

FRANK FISHER GREW UP IN ALABAMA, SON OF A PASTOR IN THE JIM CROW—ERA SOUTH.

DESPITE THEIR VASTLY DIFFERENT BACKGROUNDS, HE AND DIETRICH QUICKLY BECAME FRIENDS. DIETRICH OFTEN COMPLAINED TO FRANK ABOUT THE DULLNESS OF EVERYTHING SURROUNDING HIS FAITH IN NEW YORK. HOW HE MISSED THAT FEELING OF THE THOUSANDS WORSHIPING TOGETHER IN ROME! HE CONFIDED IN FRANK THAT HE WANTED TO EXPERIENCE GOD'S WORD AND FEEL THE LORD'S FACE SHINE UPON HIM ONCE AGAIN.

I HAVE JUST THE THING FOR YOU, MY FRIEND.

I CAN'T READ ANOTHER BOOK RIGHT NOW.

NO, NO. YOU'RE COMING WITH ME TO CHURCH.

FEW GERMANS HAD EXPERIENCED A CHURCH LIKE ABYSSINIAN. (IN FACT, BEFORE NEW YORK, DIETRICH HAD NEVER HAD A CONVERSATION WITH A BLACK PERSON BEFORE.)

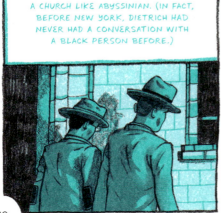

ABYSSINIAN BAPTIST CHURCH IN HARLEM

OBEYING GOD MEANS CHALLENGING INJUSTICE! YOU DON'T JUST THINK ABOUT GOD ... YOU ACT!

THIS WAS THE BEGINNING OF DIETRICH'S BAPTISM INTO BLACK CHURCH CULTURE IN AMERICA. THE PEWS ROCKED WITH ENERGY AND HOPE. DIETRICH WAS ASTONISHED! THE PREACHER— A ROLLING THUNDERCLOUD NAMED DR. ADAM CLAYTON POWELL—CAME UP INTO THE PULPIT

AND BEGAN A BOOMING MESSAGE. DR. POWELL WAS A SON OF FORMER SLAVES, AND HIS PREACHING WAS SHOT THROUGH WITH RADICAL URGENCY.

IT WAS INTOXICATING! THIS PASTOR ENCOURAGED—NO, DEMANDED—THAT THE CONGREGATION'S FAITH IN GOD BE PUT IN OPPOSITION TO THE WORLD'S EVILS. THE PEOPLE OF GOD MUST BE THE FIRST THROUGH THE BREACH WHEN FIGHTING RACISM AND INJUSTICE.

AND, OH, THE MUSIC! THE MUSIC WAS GLORIOUS.

Despite the impact that service at Abyssinian had on him (and many other services he attended there over the next year), it was a trip with Frank to visit leaders of the equality movement in Washington, D.C., that gave Dietrich a true picture of the life of a black man in America. One day on the trip, he and Frank visited a small restaurant and were abruptly told they were not allowed to dine together! For the first time, Dietrich felt a small taste of what it was like to be discriminated against. He wrote a letter to his mother about the trip.

THE SEPARATION OF WHITES FROM BLACKS IN THE SOUTHERN STATES REALLY DOES MAKE A RATHER SHAMEFUL IMPRESSION,"* SAID DIETRICH. "THE CONDITIONS ARE REALLY RATHER UNBELIEVABLE. NOT JUST SEPARATE RAILWAY CARS, TRAMWAYS, AND BUSES SOUTH OF WASHINGTON, BUT ALSO, FOR EXAMPLE WHEN I WANTED TO EAT IN A RESTAURANT WITH (FRANK), I WAS REFUSED SERVICE.*

In his studies, young Dietrich had learned about the history of slavery and racism in America. But growing up inside Germany's elite class, Dietrich had never actually experienced what it felt like to be treated like a second-class human. He was appalled to his core.

WHITE

COLORED

He continued his travels deep into the American South and couldn't believe what the nation had done to people like Frank. He wrote to his mother again, trying to process what he was seeing.

"THE WAY THE SOUTHERNERS TALK ABOUT THE [BLACKS] IS REPUGNANT ... AND THE PASTORS ARE NO BETTER THAN THE OTHERS!"*

But there was something oddly familiar about what he was seeing. It reminded him of the rhetoric of that young nationalist upstart, Adolf Hitler, and his Nazi party, who had tried to seize control of the government a few years earlier.

It was, of course, nothing to the level of what was happening in the United States.

To think that something like this kind of repulsive segregation could come to his Germany was impossible.

SO, THEN, HOW DO THE GERMAN CHURCHES RESPOND TO THIS PREJUDICE AGAINST THE JEWS?

WELL, I THINK THE GERMAN CHRISTIANS ARE NOT VERY CONCERNED WITH SUFFERINGS OUTSIDE THEIR OWN.

SOUNDS FAMILIAR.

FROM THIS POINT ON, DIETRICH COULD NO LONGER IMAGINE THEOLOGY AND FAITH AS MERE IDEAS. THEY WERE CONVICTIONS THAT DEMANDED ACTION.

JEAN

Though not as academically demanding as Dietrich was expecting, Union Theological Seminary was a true melting pot of ideas, races, and nationalities. Dietrich was not the only European student. Like the Americans Dietrich met at school, Frenchman Jean Lasserre was another former enemy of Germany in the Great War. In fact, it was the very idea of fighting for one's country that brought these two friends together. Lasserre was a strong pacifist—he believed there was no good reason for a Christian (or anyone, for that matter!) to ever fight in a war. Dietrich had always associated the ideas of "Duty to God" and "Duty to Country" as sharing the same core—how could you have one and not the other? They spent hours together debating these ideas.

DUTY TO GOD
DUTY TO COUNTRY?

On a cold evening,
the two friends went to see
a movie together. It was a new film
called "All Quiet on the Western Front." This
antiwar movie was based on a famous German novel about
the Great War. No movie had ever been made like this one before.
It didn't treat war as a glorious adventure but rather showed it as a
horrible tragedy. It showed terrified soldiers and graphic scenes of
death. In one memorable scene, a young German soldier stabs a
French soldier with his bayonet. But after his fellow soldiers retreat,
the young German, named Paul, is left in a muddy crater with
his victim for hours as the Frenchman slowly dies. Full of guilt and
shame, Paul comforts his dying enemy in the man's final moments.
After his death, Paul finds pictures of the French soldier's
family in his pocket. Dietrich and Jean, a young
German and a young Frenchman,
were moved to tears together.

They spent the rest of the night in passionate discussions about the nature of war. They wondered: Could there ever be such a thing as

... A GOOD WAR?

MARTIN LUTHER TAUGHT US THAT BECAUSE OF EVIL IN THE WORLD, WE MUST BE PREPARED TO FIGHT IT, WITH OUR COUNTRIES IF NECESSARY!

WELL, I THINK EVERY MAN IS FREE TO ACT, AND TO CHOOSE TO FOLLOW THE BIBLE INSTEAD OF FIGHTING FOR HIS HOME COUNTRY.

SO YOU WOULDN'T EVEN DEFEND YOUR OWN HOMELAND?

DIETRICH, THE CHURCH MUST BE INDEPENDENT FROM THE STATE! IT IS CALLED TO BE AN AGENT OF MORALITY, FIGHTING FOR RADICAL PEACE. IT IS NOT AS A WING OF THE ARMY.

DEFINING THE WAY THE CHURCH LOVES THE OTHER BECAME ONE OF THE MAJOR THEMES IN DIETRICH'S LIFE AND THEOLOGY. HE WOULD LATER WRITE: "THE CHURCH IS ONLY THE CHURCH WHEN IT EXISTS FOR OTHERS ... NOT DOMINATING, BUT HELPING AND SERVING. IT MUST TELL MEN OF EVERY CALLING WHAT IT MEANS TO LIVE FOR CHRIST, TO EXIST FOR OTHERS."*

Dietrich left this conversation uncertain of his own conclusions about war. Jean had told him to reread Jesus's Sermon on the Mount, which talks about how we should love and care for others. And it was at this point that Dietrich became convinced that he must see the church as his friends Frank and Jean did, as a revolutionary force. But this revolution carried with it both a call to civil action and a mission of radical peace that held no ties to nation or state.

In 1931, Dietrich began his voyage back home to Germany. As a parting gift, Frank gave him a copy of "American Negro Spirituals"— a songbook Dietrich had with him for the rest of his life.

His year in America had given Dietrich a new foundation. His theology had been transformed from thought into action, the creation of something he called

"CIVIL COURAGE."

Dietrich was beginning to separate the idea of his own country's glory from the glory of God, but the very opposite thing was happening in Germany. The teetering country had grown desperate in the decade since the end of the Great War. The people were hungry for a vision of triumph, conquest, and rebirth.

The gregarious nationalist Adolf Hitler had been gaining moderate support before Dietrich had left for New York. He was telling a story to the German people that they were eager to hear—a hopeful prophecy of German ascension. Hitler even used the name of God and the German churches to help sell this story. Hitler proclaimed that the Germans were a special people, destined by God to overthrow their enemies. When the Great Depression arrived in Germany in 1929, things had gone from bad to worse. After a decade of want and hunger, the German people were eager to embrace anyone who promised change.

Slowly but steadily, Hitler's promises of wealth and revenge found a home in the heart of the German people. They had little inkling of what we know today: that he was a wolf in sheep's clothing. The hidden monster before them would eventually consume half the world in war. But in that moment, he gave the people hope. Indeed, by 1932, the Nazis had become the largest political party in Germany.

Throughout the Nazi rise to power, Hitler relied on his private militia: a personal army of soldiers that gave his ideas the visual impression of power. His storm troopers wore distinctive brown shirts with red armbands, and they paraded around Nazi rallies with brooding menace.

Since 1919, when Germany abandoned the monarchy, the new cabinet-style government had floundered. In the new system, the people elected a president every seven years. Then the president appointed a chancellor to lead the many government departments from within the elected parliament, called the Reichstag. But there was a flaw. There were too many political parties to get a clear consensus in the Reichstag. It was difficult to pass any kind of laws or legislation. Nothing could get done! Years of this revolving-door leadership had taken its toll on the nation's confidence. Many of the people longed for a kaiser to return and unify the country. Hitler was a cunning manipulator of this uncertainty.

He lay crouched in the brush, waiting for just the right moment to pounce on his wounded prey.

HITLER WAS OBSESSED WITH WOLVES AND OFTEN USED THEM AS A SYMBOL FOR HIMSELF. THE NAME ADOLF MEANS "NOBLE WOLF." DURING HIS EARLY CAREER HE WOULD SOMETIMES REFER TO HIMSELF AS "HERR WOLF." HE EVEN NAMED ONE OF HIS GERMAN SHEPHERDS "WOLF."

That moment came in early January 1933, when the existing German government collapsed from within once again. The chancellor stepped down in disgrace. This was Hitler's opportunity. With vast popular support behind him, Hitler pressed the beloved German president, a mustachioed old war hero named Paul von Hindenburg, to install him as the new chancellor. Hitler's lobbying worked. The 85-year-old president appointed Hitler to the office as part of a deal with his rival politicians who felt this appointment would mollify Hitler and keep his Nazi party under government control. (It wouldn't.)

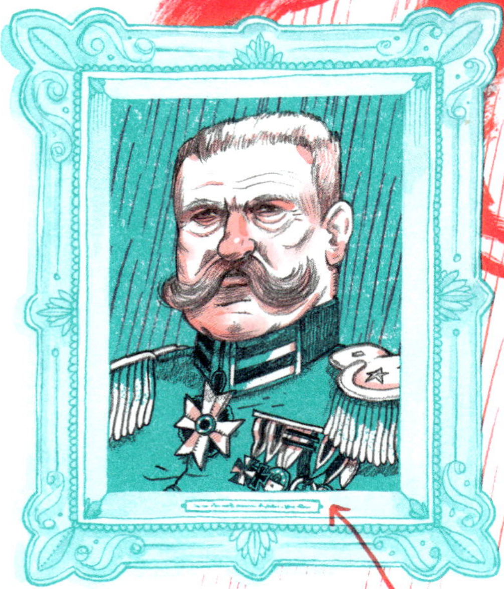

THE PRESIDENT'S FULL NAME AND TITLE WAS QUITE LONG: FIELD MARSHAL PAUL LUDWIG HANS ANTON VON BENECKENDORFF UND VON HINDENBURG!

SOMEHOW, ADOLF HITLER, A MAN WHO WAS ONCE CONVICTED OF HIGH TREASON AND SEEN AS A POLITICAL OUTCAST, WAS LEGALLY GIVEN GERMANY'S CHANCELLORSHIP ON JANUARY 30, 1933. FROM THIS POINT FORWARD, GERMANY'S COURSE WAS BEING SET BY A MADMAN. HITLER WAS STEERING THE GREAT GERMAN GALLEON STRAIGHT INTO

A HURRICANE!

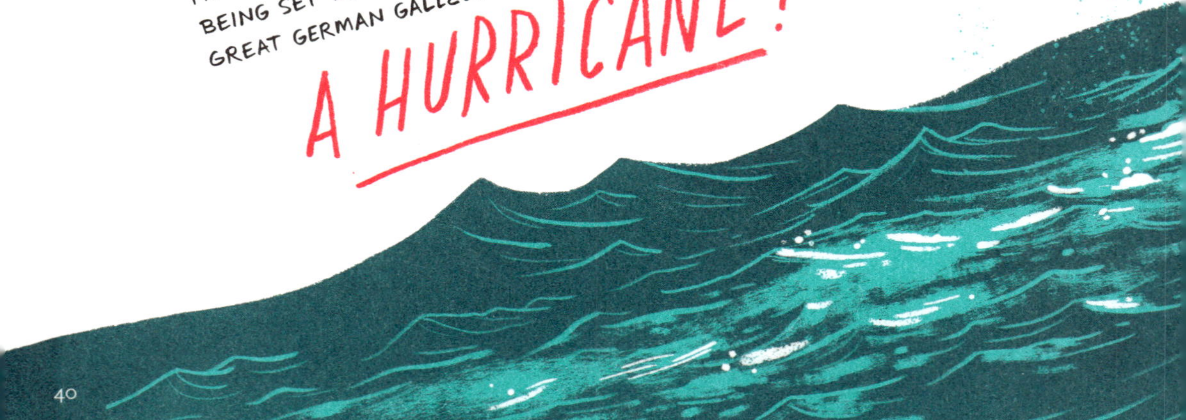

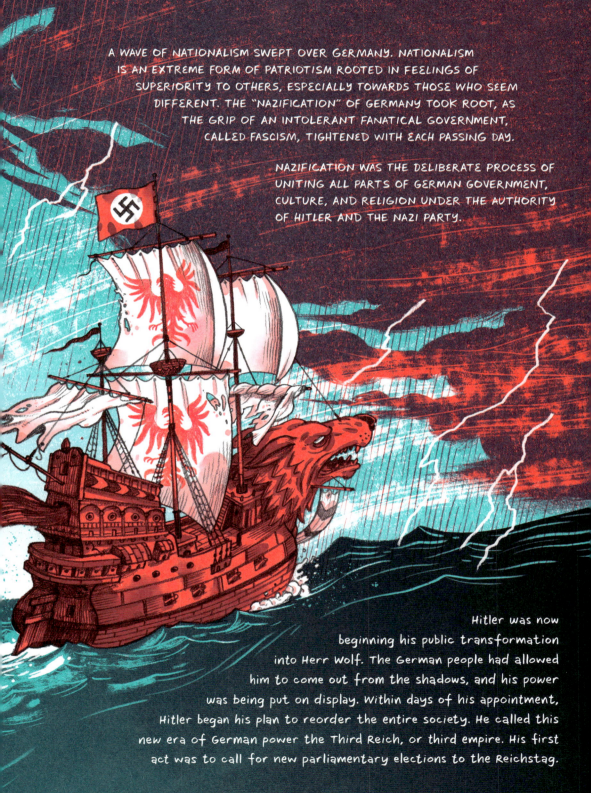

A WAVE OF NATIONALISM SWEPT OVER GERMANY. NATIONALISM IS AN EXTREME FORM OF PATRIOTISM ROOTED IN FEELINGS OF SUPERIORITY TO OTHERS, ESPECIALLY TOWARDS THOSE WHO SEEM DIFFERENT. THE "NAZIFICATION" OF GERMANY TOOK ROOT, AS THE GRIP OF AN INTOLERANT FANATICAL GOVERNMENT, CALLED FASCISM, TIGHTENED WITH EACH PASSING DAY.

NAZIFICATION WAS THE DELIBERATE PROCESS OF UNITING ALL PARTS OF GERMAN GOVERNMENT, CULTURE, AND RELIGION UNDER THE AUTHORITY OF HITLER AND THE NAZI PARTY.

Hitler was now beginning his public transformation into Herr Wolf. The German people had allowed him to come out from the shadows, and his power was being put on display. Within days of his appointment, Hitler began his plan to reorder the entire society. He called this new era of German power the Third Reich, or third empire. His first act was to call for new parliamentary elections to the Reichstag.

On February 27, 1933, just a few days before the new election on March 5, a mysterious fire broke out in the Reichstag, the massive home of the German legislature. The entire building was gutted. As if they had had a premonition, the Nazi party leaders were on the scene within moments of the news. They instantly pinned the blame for the entire plot on a faction of radical communists who they claimed were eager to overthrow the German republic. (Today, many historians believe the blaze was actually set by Hitler's Nazis themselves!) This trauma was a perfect excuse to cajole old President Hindenburg to expand Hitler's powers.

Indeed, the very next day, Hitler persuaded President Hindenburg to suspend sections of the German constitution. The grand-sounding "Reich President's Edict for Protection of People and State" took away all civil liberties throughout the entire country, which included the rights of free speech, a free press, and free assembly. The Nazi propaganda machine stoked the fears of the people, reminding them that a vote for Nazis in the upcoming election was a vote for protection from a communist revolution, which many feared.

Not surprisingly, the election was a Nazi victory. The people's fears pushed out the smaller parties, and the Nazis won just enough seats to gain control of the parliament. At the end of March, Hitler's Nazi party in the Reichstag passed a law that, ironically, made that very Reichstag irrelevant! The "Enabling Act," passed on March 23, 1933, suspended the legislative process, giving Hitler the power to make laws on his own! Within weeks, Hitler had dismantled the German constitution and made himself nearly untouchable by the law. This single act was the legal linchpin on which Hitler's future dictatorship was founded.

HITLER BEGAN CALLING HIMSELF **DER FÜHRER** (THE LEADER).

It was more than just a formal title. It was intended to make it seem as if God had made him a savior to the people. But he wasn't a leader who served the people. He let it be known that it was the people's duty to serve him!

DURING THIS TIME, HITLER WOULD BRAZENLY WALK AROUND CARRYING A RIDING WHIP

In a democracy, leaders are given power by the people who elect them. But Hitler claimed that his power as "The Führer" was bestowed by God himself. In his view, he had been appointed as Germany's savior. So Hitler's leadership was a divine appointment and could not be challenged by anyone without challenging God! (Very convenient.)

Hitler knew he would need German churches to support this claim. Always a cunning manipulator, he wore the mask of a Christian in public. (In fact, he hated Christianity and often griped to his inner circle about how much he hated its principles of forgiveness and self-sacrifice.) But he convinced leaders of the churches that he should be head of both the German state AND the German church. The Führer created the

REICH CHURCH,

the official church of the Nazi Party and true religious authority of Germany. Hitler was working to bring every part of German life under his control, something he called "GLEICHSCHALTUNG"— the coordination of everything to be in line with Nazi thinking and policies. The great cathedrals of Germany were now wreathed in the symbol of the swastika—it was, fittingly, a broken cross. Hitler would soon break the German Christian church itself.

DURING THIS TIME, SOME GERMAN CHRISTMAS TREES WERE TOPPED WITH SWASTIKAS INSTEAD OF STARS.

The downtrodden people of Germany adored this triumphant new version of Christianity. No more did they have to pray for their enemies or "turn the other cheek." This new church that Hitler created was strong and full of aggressive values. No longer weak, the church would finally be dominant and pure! It was a church that was pledged to the Führer and then to God, in that order.

Hitler revealed something of his ultimate aims when he passed the "Aryan Paragraph," part of the "Law for Restoration of the Civil Service" in April 1933, only a few months after becoming chancellor.

Hitler had rightly predicted that the soft underbelly of the German church would not offer resistance. Though some church leaders labeled the proposal as "unfortunate," the Aryan Paragraph was accepted by most pastors throughout Germany. The entire country, and now even the church's leadership, had fallen under Hitler's intoxicating spell.

THE ARYAN PARAGRAPH

THIS PRONOUNCEMENT REQUIRED THE REMOVAL OF ANYONE WITH NON-ARYAN OR JEWISH HERITAGE FROM ANY PART OF CIVIL SERVICE IN GERMANY, INCLUDING THE CHURCH! HITLER USED THE WORD ARYAN TO MEAN "OF PURE GERMAN DESCENT." THIS LABEL WAS AN INEXACT BUT EASY MEANS TO MARK GERMAN MINORITIES AS AN ALIEN THREAT.

THIS ACT WAS HIS FIRST STEP TOWARD THE IDEAS HE HAD LAID OUT IN HIS BOOK "MEIN KAMPF": TO STRIP ALL JEWISH GERMANS OF THEIR CIVIL RIGHTS. LATER THAT SAME YEAR, HITLER EXPANDED THE CLAUSE SO THAT EVEN THOSE MARRIED TO JEWS WOULD BE BANNED FROM CIVIL SERVICE.

GERMANY NEEDED SOMEONE TO WAKE IT UP!

CHAPTER 3

GOD IS MY FÜHRER

DIETRICH LEANED CLOSE TO THE MICROPHONE

and took a deep breath. His voice was calm and confident in every word.

WHEN A LEADER ALLOWS HIMSELF TO SUCCUMB TO THE WISHES OF THOSE HE LEADS, OF THOSE WHO WILL ALWAYS SEEK TO TURN HIM INTO THEIR IDOL, THE IMAGE OF THE LEADER WILL GRADUALLY BECOME THE IMAGE OF THE "MIS-LEADER."* LEADERS OR OFFICES WHICH SET THEMSELVES UP AS GODS MOCK GOD AND THE INDIVIDUAL WHO STANDS ALONE BEFORE HIM, AND MUST PERISH.*

SUDDENLY, JUST AS HE WAS REACHING THE DRAMATIC CRESCENDO OF HIS ARGUMENT, THE MICROPHONE WENT DEAD.

HELLO?

DIETRICH LOOKED INTO THE BOOTH AND SAW THE RADIO ENGINEER FUMBLING WITH THE CONTROLS. FINALLY, HE CONCLUDED:

WE'VE BEEN CUT OFF!

THIS VERY RADIO ADDRESS WAS MADE JUST TWO DAYS AFTER HITLER BECAME GERMANY'S CHANCELLOR.

DIETRICH'S LECTURE WAS BROADCAST ON BERLIN'S RUNDFUNK (RADIO) DURING THE BUSY HOURS OF THE EVENING WHEN EVERYONE AT THE CAFÉS AND BARS WOULD HAVE HEARD HIM. DIETRICH HAD TAKEN TO THE AIRWAVES IN THE CALCULATED MANNER OF A THEOLOGIAN, AND WAS CONSTRUCTING AN ARGUMENT AGAINST THE IDEA OF

THE FÜHRER.

IN THE MESSAGE, HE ARGUED THAT THE TRUE POWER OF A LEADER CAME FROM HIS WILLINGNESS TO SERVE THE PEOPLE. THOUGH NEVER DIRECTLY MENTIONING HITLER BY NAME, HE WAS BRAVELY IDENTIFYING ...

THE FÜHRER

NOT JUST AS A THREAT TO GERMANY, BUT AS A SPIRITUAL DANGER: A FALSE IDOL OF WORSHIP.

DIETRICH HATED THE WAY HITLER SPOKE IN PUBLIC, WAVING HIS ARMS, SHOUTING AND SPITTING AS HE TALKED (THIS IS CALLED "HISTRIONICS"). WHENEVER DIETRICH SPOKE, HE ALWAYS MADE SURE TO BE CALM, CLEAR, AND KIND.

It had been eighteen months since Dietrich had returned to Germany from America. He joined the faculty at Berlin University, teaching theology. But it wasn't until that moment at the microphone that young Dietrich was set on a collision course with the Third Reich. To this day, no one knows why Dietrich's radio signal was cut abruptly. Some suspect it was the newly elected Nazis already exerting their control over public speech. In February 1933, the Nazis created a secret police force, called the Gestapo for just this purpose. The Gestapo became a notorious agency designed to root out disloyalty through intimidation and outright violence.

THE GESTAPO'S ACTUAL NAME WAS GEHEIME STAATSPOLIZEI. A POSTAL CLERK WHO WAS TIRED OF WRITING THE LONG TITLE GAVE THEM THE ABBREVIATED NAME:

GE-STA-PO.

Even Dietrich might not have suspected foul play. At the moment, he was mostly annoyed that he couldn't finish his final conclusions on the air. After the broadcast, the next months were nothing less than a seismic upheaval of German society. Dietrich's family, like many others, had assumed the annoyance of the Nazi rhetoric was a passing phase— but the daily routine was cracking under the weight of Hitler's new authority. Even more troubling to Dietrich, the German church itself was also buckling.

First they accepted the Aryan Paragraph, then pastors began to wear the  distinctive bronze eagle (a symbol of the Nazi Party, which had once topped the storm troopers' rally banners) on their coat lapels. Soon enough they even began baptizing babies to Hitler instead of God! Some pastors would even end their services not with the Christian Doxology, but with Hitler's official salute, called the Hitlergruss, and a shout of

HEIL HITLER! (WHICH MEANS "HAIL HITLER").

The Christian faith had been shipwrecked on the rocks of Hitler's Reich. Thanks to his travels, Dietrich had seen things that many Germans had not. He understood something of the church outside the borders of Germany. Rome had shown Dietrich the spiritual power of community. Frank Fisher had shown him what persecution felt like in Harlem and in the American South. Dietrich wasn't fooled by the faulty premise of the Aryan Paragraph. He knew it wasn't created to protect the church, instead it was a vulgar discrimination. But what could he do? How could the church—the true church, not the one dressed up in Nazi flags—respond? Dietrich did what any good theologian would do ...

I MUST WRITE ABOUT THIS!

Two weeks after the Aryan Paragraph was passed in April 1933, Dietrich published a public paper called "The Church and the Jewish Question." This paper was a blistering attack on the Nazi idols being built in the heart of Germany. Those in the church who were going to oppose Hitler's anti-Jewish policies (what he called 'The Jewish Question') needed a playbook for resistance in the name of God, and that's just what he gave them. He wrote that the church should "continually ask the state whether its action can be justified. ..."* After this opening query, he defined three possible ways the church can respond toward a hostile state:

1. QUESTION THE STATE AND ITS METHODS.
A TRUE CHURCH MUST PROTECT ITSELF AND REJECT GOVERNMENT ENCROACHMENT ON ITS BELIEFS.

2. AID THE VICTIMS OF STATE ACTION.
THE CHURCH HAS AN UNCONDITIONAL OBLIGATION TO THE VICTIMS OF ANY ORDERING OF SOCIETY.

3. STRIKE BACK.
IT IS NOT ENOUGH JUST TO BANDAGE THE VICTIMS UNDER THE WHEEL—BUT TO PUT A SPOKE IN THE WHEEL ITSELF!*

THE JEWISH QUESTION TROUBLES THE CHURCH VERY MUCH AND HERE EVEN THE MOST INTELLIGENT PEOPLE HAVE ENTIRELY LOST THEIR HEADS AND THEIR BIBLES OVER IT!*

Dietrich somehow saw the future. Like a true Biblical prophet, he aimed to shout it from the rooftops—hoping to wake a sleeping nation. But the church authorities would not hear him. They begged him to stop causing trouble and to fall in line with the Nazi regulations. Dietrich just could not believe their lack of compassion for the Jewish people. As Dietrich had witnessed in Harlem, a real faith demanded action or it was no faith at all. He knew a church unwilling to stand up for suffering Jews would eventually stand for nothing. As he pointed out, under the Aryan Paragraph, Saint Peter, Saint Paul, and Jesus himself would not be allowed inside a German Christian church!

His strident opposition had made him an outcast in most high-society circles. Dietrich was a stubborn individual once he set his mind to a task. Among his fellow Berlin theology professors, he was now an official pest. Even those who shared his beliefs were wavering against the monolith of Nazi power. The pastors he admired began to ask if a compromise would be better for the long-term health of the church.

IF YOU BOARD THE WRONG TRAIN, IT IS NO USE RUNNING ALONG THE CORRIDOR IN THE OPPOSITE DIRECTION!*

In his frustration, Dietrich left Germany to take a post in London, England, as the pastor to a German-speaking congregation. It was a hasty decision. But he was sick of marinating in Germany's troubles.

Despite being physically absent from the fight, he didn't waste his time in England. Dietrich joined the effort of a group of resistance pastors back home led by the great German theologian Martin Niemöller, to create the Pastors' Emergency League. They opposed the Aryan Paragraph and the Nazification of the church. Martin had initially supported Hitler's rise to power, until the creation of the Aryan Paragraph roused him to action. Six thousand German pastors eventually became members. It was during this time that Dietrich came into contact with George Bell, the English bishop of Chichester. George was a well-respected church leader who had high connections inside the British government. In a few years, Bishop Bell would become one of Dietrich's primary contacts as a spy working against the Third Reich. While living in England, Dietrich traveled quite often across mainland Europe and Scandinavia, working outside Germany to rally ecumenical support for a theological stand against the Nazi church. In May 1934, Dietrich returned to Germany to attend a major meeting of the Pastors' Emergency League. In the town of Barmen, the league officially became the "Confessing Church" with a document called ...

GEORGE BELL

54

THE BARMEN DECLARATION.

This was a kind of "Declaration of Independence" for the rebellion. It was a bold act of war against the Nazi "Reich Church." The document outlined the heresy of anti-Jewish policies and the false doctrine of Führer worship. Prior to the declaration, Dietrich had written to non-German theologians in London begging for more global support of the German struggle. Before returning to Germany, he wrote:

> TO DELAY OR FAIL TO MAKE DECISIONS MAY BE MORE SINFUL THAN TO MAKE WRONG DECISIONS OUT OF FAITH AND LOVE. *

But the English were skeptical of such a bold stance against Hitler. When the Barmen Declaration went public, the Confessing Church became the first public religious opposition to Nazi policies of discrimination. It also made the Confessing Church, and Dietrich, a target for Hitler's fury. Even from across the English Channel, Dietrich could sense the angry tentacles of the Third Reich were coming for him.

BUT BEFORE HITLER COULD DEAL WITH THE ANNOYING CHRISTIAN REBELS, HE HAD SOME MORE PRESSING BUSINESS TO ATTEND TO.

IN the months following Hitler's rise, the storm troopers' display of power had become more brazen and their reach more brutal. They would savagely beat anyone on the streets who didn't give the Nazi salute as their parades passed by. They would place these rebellious citizens into "protective custody," a much nicer term than the reality. Many Germans were imprisoned merely for opposing Nazi ideas. Berlin, the German capital, had as many as fifty of these improvised prisons, which also served as torture centers. Of course, frequent targets of storm trooper violence were the Jews. Hitler's anti-Jewish rhetoric had practically made it legal to beat and torture Jews in public for no reason.

It was becoming clear that Hitler, even as the chancellor of Germany, was not in control of his zealots. The ranks of the storm troopers were now millions strong, led by Ernst Röhm, one of Hitler's ambitious toadies. Röhm warned he wouldn't muzzle the storm troopers until he was in control of a new unified Reichswehr (German army) as its defense minister.

THE GERMAN ARMY WAS LIMITED TO 100,000 MEN BY THE TREATY OF VERSAILLES. IN CONTRAST, BY 1934, THE SA (STORM TROOPERS) HAD NEARLY 3 MILLION MEN.

The sitting military leaders had distrusted Hitler, but the idea of a crude hooligan like Röhm and his roughneck tactics leading the entire Reichswehr was a complete abomination to them. The tensions among the army, Hitler, and the storm troopers threatened the entire government.

Hitler was now caught in a vise between the fear that President Hindenburg would depose him because of this dangerous tension with the military and his loyalty to Röhm and the support of his storm troopers. The portly old Great War veteran Hindenburg had the constitutional authority to appoint a new chancellor at any time. If Hitler's Nazi Party appeared unstable and mutinous, Hindenburg had the power to quickly dump Hitler from the chancellorship. Ironically, the strength of Hitler's storm troopers, which had ushered Hitler into office, was becoming a major threat to his hold on the reins of power.

57

PRESIDENT HINDENBURG

THE REICHSTAG

NOT UNDER HITLER'S CONTROL

RÖHM

THE SA (STORM TROOPERS)

REICHSWEHR (ARMY)

UNDER HITLER'S CONTROL

CHANCELLOR HITLER

THE GESTAPO

THE SS

In the summer of 1934, President Hindenburg fell deathly ill. Hitler saw his opening. Now that one of the last pillars of German power was teetering like a German spruce ... HITLER COULDN'T RESIST A FINAL VICIOUS CHOP.

Hitler's blow came in the form of an audacious secret killing spree—a bloodbath that came to be known as

THE NIGHT OF LONG KNIVES!

On June 29, 1934, 200 (possibly more) leaders of the storm troopers and opponents to Hitler's reign were executed in their homes by the Gestapo. The killings were also carried out by henchmen from the Gestapo and Hitler's new elite fighting force, called the SCHUTZSTAFFEL, or the SS. The victims of these attacks were not shadowy rebels but politicians, writers, and even Hitler's own men. Hitler ordered the killing of two army generals and the leader of the storm troopers, Ernst Röhm himself! This savage betrayal would centralize his powers and take away any threat of being deposed. Hitler had made a quiet deal with the army: Hitler would eliminate the storm troopers, but only if the army would support him for the presidency once Hindenburg died.

BUT HOW COULD A SITTING CHANCELLOR GET AWAY WITH ORDERING HUNDREDS OF MURDERS?

As Hitler addressed the nation on July 13, 1934, he explained everything: He had saved Germany from a group of traitors who were threatening the Reich. These members of the storm troopers, along with many others, were plotting to seize the government. Hitler had no choice, he reasoned, but to declare war on them first. Yes, he had acted rashly (and outside the legal system), but it was all in the service of German security.

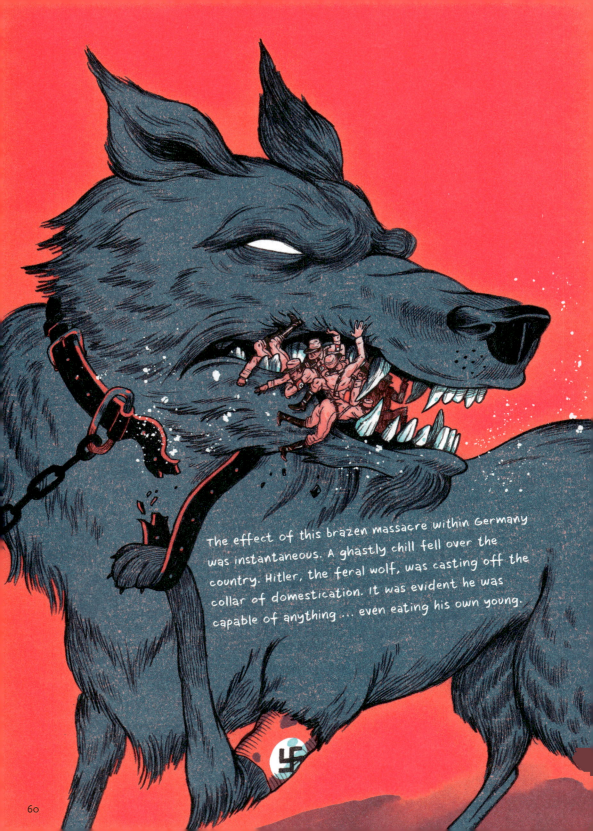

The effect of this brazen massacre within Germany was instantaneous. A ghastly chill fell over the country. Hitler, the feral wolf, was casting off the collar of domestication. It was evident he was capable of anything ... even eating his own young.

The old president, Hindenburg, died on August 2, 1934, leaving a drafty hole in the leadership structure. Hitler bravely suggested that after the loss of President Hindenburg, he alone should occupy the roles of both chancellor AND president. Still wanting to keep up the appearances of a good leader to the rest of the world, Hitler insisted that a vote would be held to confirm the country's wishes on a sensitive topic. In a hasty election, Hitler won in a landslide, gaining 90 percent of the ballots cast. (Hitler probably didn't even have to cheat with the ballot counting that much to win this election.) Hitler was now both head of state and head of government. The title of president was abolished. Hitler was now "Führer and Reich chancellor."

THE GENERALS HAD TAKEN A TERRIBLE POLITICAL GAMBLE. BY MAKING COMMON CAUSE WITH HITLER (AND SACRIFICING TWO OF THEIR OWN GENERALS IN THE PURGE), THEY LOST THE MORAL AUTHORITY TO PUBLICALLY QUESTION HITLER'S AMBITIONS. WITH THE DEAL, THEY SOUGHT TO PROTECT THE ARMY'S POWER FROM NAZI CONTROL, BUT THEY HAD DONE THE OPPOSITE. AS PART OF THE DEAL, HITLER CLOSED THIS LOOPHOLE BY DEMANDING THE ARMY WOULD NO LONGER SWEAR AN OATH OF LOYALTY TO GERMANY, BUT TO HITLER HIMSELF!

WITH THIS SIMPLE OATH OF ALLEGIANCE, HITLER HAD SHACKLED THE GENERALS WITH THEIR OWN OUTDATED CODE OF HONOR. AS PROUD GERMAN SOLDIERS, THEY WERE NOW HONOR BOUND TO SERVE THEIR FÜHRER. ANY SMOLDERING HOPE OF REMOVING ADOLF HITLER FROM POWER THROUGH TRADITIONAL DEMOCRACY WAS TOTALLY EXTINGUISHED. GERMANY WAS MAROONED WITH AN

OMNIPRESENT DICTATOR.

CHAPTER 4
THE DECISION

IN 1934, WHILE THE WORLD WAS STILL FIVE YEARS AWAY FROM TOTAL WAR, DIETRICH WAS PREPARING YOUNG MEN TO FIGHT IN A DIFFERENT WAY.

THE YOUNG PREACHER HAD RETURNED

from London to open his own rebel seminary, supported by the Confessing Church, in northern Germany on the Baltic coast. At first on the beaches of Zingst, then inland near the tiny town of Finkenwalde, he enlisted about two dozen young men and taught them how to preach, without Nazi censorship. He hoped that with enough trained pastors, they could undercut the popular support for Hitler's heresy against the Jews. His efforts were funded by secret patrons like Ruth von Kleist-Retzow. Ruth, a strong-willed aristocrat who was sympathetic to the cause, was sometimes called the "Matriarch of the Resistance." She adored Dietrich.

To study with Bonhoeffer was dangerous—it was a clear mark of dissent. It signaled to the government authorities that you might be trouble. Life at Finkenwalde was sparse but full of life and love. Bonhoeffer was an odd professor. As a teacher, he was demanding, like his father. But as a leader, he had an unpredictable streak of whimsy. Dietrich would often cancel classes suddenly to take a day trip to the nearby beach dunes. Or he would postpone the day's activities for a rigorous table tennis tournament! (He was quite good.) Ever since his childhood, Dietrich had been a natural musician. Now, using his beloved songbook from Frank Fisher, he taught the young seminarians (and frequent visitor Ruth) hymns and spirituals like "Swing Low, Sweet Chariot."

THE REBEL SEMINARY FIRST MET ON THE BEACHES OF ZINGST.

ALTHOUGH THE SEMINARY WAS ILLEGAL, DIETRICH AND HIS STUDENTS STUDIED AND PRAYED IN RELATIVE PEACE. THEY WERE A SMALL ENOUGH GROUP TO AVOID DETECTION BY THE GESTAPO. BUT THERE WAS A CLOUD HANGING OVER THEIR HEADS. AS YOUNG MEN IN A COUNTRY GROWING MORE MILITANT BY THE DAY, CONSCRIPTION, DRAFTED INTO MILITARY SERVICE, WAS POSSIBLE AT ANY MOMENT.

At Finkenwalde, Dietrich met Eberhard Bethge, who was one of his students and eventually his best friend. Because he had been a theological wunderkind at such a young age, Dietrich wasn't that much older than his students. These two would exchange hundreds of letters over the next ten years.

Thanks to his friendship with Jean Lasserre, Dietrich had come to believe in pacifism. Well, it wasn't quite as simple as that. At the very least, he no longer felt it was a Christian's duty to fight for his country. He never required his students to believe the same as he did in this matter, because he wasn't sure this conviction was always true. What if a man were to refuse to fight, and as result the government would imprison or even execute his family? Wouldn't it be wrong to refuse to fight in that case? He understood how his students could feel very different from him about serving in the German army.

In fact, nearly all his students disagreed with his belief in pacifism. They believed, even though they hated Hitler's Nazi policies, that if Germany was attacked, it was their duty to defend it. Each one of them, including their pacifist professor, would have to make a choice soon enough.

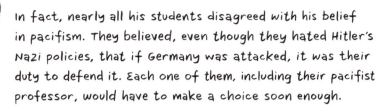

THE GERMAN MILITARY, EVEN THOUGH IT FOUGHT ON BEHALF OF THE NAZIS, WAS SEPARATE FROM THE NAZI PARTY ITSELF. THE COLLECTION OF ARMED FORCES, RENAMED IN 1935 AS THE WEHRMACHT, CONTAINED THE ARMY, THE HEER; THE NAVY, THE KRIEGSMARINE; AND THE AIR FORCE, THE LUFTWAFFE. MOST GERMANS UNDERSTOOD THE ARMY AS IDEOLOGICALLY DISTINCT FROM THE NAZI PARTY DURING THIS TIME.

The rebel seminary of the Confessing Church at Finkenwalde was able to avoid catching the eye of the Gestapo for about a year and a half. During this time, Dietrich wrote two classic works of Christian theology,

"THE COST OF DISCIPLESHIP" and "LIFE TOGETHER."

Both of these works further explored his long-debated question: "What, exactly, is the church?" and "How does the church love 'the other'?" But in the shadowy corners of Berlin, on the eve of the city's 1936 Olympic Games, the noose was beginning to tighten on the brothers of the Confessing Church.

EVEN THE PUBLIC SEEMED TO BE TURNING AGAINST THE REBELLIOUS CHURCH. DIETRICH FOUND A CARD WITH THIS OMINOUS POEM IN A BERLIN BOOKSHOP:

"AFTER THE END OF THE OLYMPIADE WE'LL BEAT THE CC [CONFESSING CHURCH] TO MARMALADE. THEN WE'LL CHUCK OUT THE JEW, THE CC WILL END TOO."*

WITHOUT MUCH WARNING, HITLER'S REICH STRUCK AT THE HEART OF THE THEOLOGICAL REBELLION.

In July 1936, as Berlin's triumphant propaganda machine celebrated hosting the Olympic Games, two confessing Church members were arrested under a law that made any association with non-Nazi churches illegal. The arrests would only continue to grow.

HITLER HELD THE 1936 OLYMPIC GAMES IN BERLIN TO SEND A CLEAR MESSAGE TO THE WORLD: THE FUTURE TRIUMPH OF GERMANY! HITLER WANTED TO SHOWCASE THE GERMAN'S SUPERIORITY TO THE OTHER RACES OF THE WORLD. INDEED, THE GAMES WERE A GLITTERY SPECTACLE THAT CAPTIVATED THE GLOBAL MEDIA. BUT A YOUNG AFRICAN AMERICAN NAMED JESSE OWENS STOLE SOME OF HITLER'S GLORY. THE BRILLIANT SPRINTER BEAT OUT THE GERMAN SUPERSTAR LUZ LONG IN THE LONG JUMP, RUINING HITLER'S PERFECT NARRATIVE OF GERMAN DOMINANCE (ESPECIALLY CONSIDERING OWENS WAS BOTH BLACK AND AN AMERICAN!). OWENS WENT ON TO WIN FOUR GOLD MEDALS IN THE 1936 GAMES, SOMETHING OF AN ABOMINATION TO HITLER AND HIS INNER CIRCLE OF STRIDENT RACISTS.

THROUGHOUT 1937, THE PLIGHT OF THE REBELLIOUS CHURCH BECAME MUCH MORE DESPERATE. HITLER, THROUGH THE REICH CHURCH, BANNED ANYONE FROM PUBLICLY PRAYING FOR MEMBERS OF THE REBELLION. CHURCHES COULD NO LONGER COLLECT OFFERINGS FOR THE CONFESSING CHURCH. THEN CAME MORE ARRESTS. BY THE END OF THE YEAR, NEARLY 800 OF THE MOST OUTSPOKEN MEMBERS OF THE CONFESSING CHURCH WERE TAKEN INTO STATE CUSTODY.

HERMANN STÖHR, A FRIEND OF DIETRICH'S, WAS SEIZED BY THE SS. HERMANN WAS EVENTUALLY EXECUTED FOR REFUSING TO JOIN THE ARMY.

HERMANN STÖHR

JULY 1, 1937
DIETRICH AND EBERHARD PAID A VISIT TO MARTIN NIEMÖLLER.

SHAKEN BY THE NAZI CRACKDOWN, THEY SOUGHT TO MEET THE PROMINENT PREACHER NIEMÖLLER (WITH WHOM DIETRICH HAD FOUNDED THE PASTORS' EMERGENCY LEAGUE) AND PLOT A WAY FORWARD. BUT MARTIN'S DISTRAUGHT WIFE ANSWERED THE DOOR. THE MINISTER HAD BEEN ARRESTED JUST MINUTES BEFORE THEY ARRIVED!

SUDDENLY A BLACK GESTAPO MERCEDES SCREECHED TO A HALT IN FRONT OF THE PARSONAGE! DIETRICH AND EBERHARD TRIED TO ESCAPE OUT THE BACK BUT WERE APPREHENDED BY GESTAPO AGENTS.

THEY WERE HELD FOR SEVEN HOURS WHILE THE GESTAPO TORE APART THE WALLS AND FURNITURE, LOOKING FOR HIDDEN MONEY DESIGNATED FOR THE CONFESSING CHURCH. FINALLY, THE GESTAPO'S FASTIDIOUS NATURE PAID OFF:

THEY FOUND 30,000 MARKS BELONGING TO THE PASTORS' EMERGENCY LEAGUE IN A SAFE HIDDEN BEHIND A PAINTING IN THE HOUSE!

THROUGH SOME MIRACLE, (OR THE GESTAPO'S IGNORANCE OF WHO THEY REALLY WERE) DIETRICH AND EBERHARD WERE RELEASED THAT NIGHT ...

MARTIN NIEMÖLLER SPOKE
THESE FAMOUS WORDS ABOUT
THIS TIME IN GERMANY:

FIRST THEY CAME FOR THE
SOCIALISTS,
AND I DID NOT SPEAK OUT—
BECAUSE I WAS NOT A SOCIALIST.

THEN THEY CAME FOR THE
TRADE UNIONISTS,
AND I DID NOT SPEAK OUT—
BECAUSE I WAS NOT A
TRADE UNIONIST.

THEN THEY CAME FOR THE JEWS,
AND I DID NOT SPEAK OUT—
BECAUSE I WAS NOT A JEW.

THEN THEY CAME FOR ME
AND THERE WAS NO ONE LEFT
TO SPEAK FOR ME.*

... but not Martin Niemöller. His
family assumed he was taken for a
brief questioning, but he wasn't seen
again for eight years, until after
the war.

MARTIN NIEMÖLLER

After this close call, Dietrich remained elusive. As punishment, the
Reich banned him from entering Berlin for any reason, even to visit
his family. While on break between terms in the fall of 1937, Dietrich
was away traveling and got an urgent call from Finkenwalde:
The seminary had been seized by the Gestapo ...

... AND WOULD NEVER REOPEN.

Finkenwalde
Seminary

DIETRICH DIDN'T KNOW THAT INSIDE
THE NAZI HEADQUARTERS, HITLER WAS
PREPARING A NEW ASSAULT THAT WENT
WELL BEYOND THE CONFESSING CHURCH.

Ever since the deal Hitler made to oust Röhm and his storm troopers, the army generals had seen Hitler as an ambitious but shrewd leader on the rise. This dramatically changed on November 5, 1937. In a private four-hour meeting with his top generals, Hitler revealed he had created a secret plan: It was a plan for nothing less than total German domination.

AND IT WOULD BEGIN IMMEDIATELY!

• THE FIRST ITEM ON HIS LIST: GERMANY WOULD ANNEX AUSTRIA, HITLER'S HOMELAND. AUSTRIA WAS ONCE PART OF THE LARGER GERMAN EMPIRE, AND THIS WAS A BRAZEN LAND GRAB.

• AFTER AUSTRIA, HE WOULD INVADE NEIGHBORING CZECHOSLOVAKIA.

• THEN HE WOULD MARCH ON POLAND.

• THEN BELGIUM AND HOLLAND …
• THEN DENMARK, NORWAY …
• THEN FRANCE …
• THEN, ACROSS THE CHANNEL, TO ENGLAND …

WORLD DOMINATION

CLAIMING THEM ALL FOR GERMANY!

Many of the generals in the meeting were flabbergasted. They looked at one another in horror. For this, Hitler would bring the world's anger down upon Germany again! They were being led into a war they were not ready to fight … a war they would surely lose.

THERE ARE LIMITS TO ONE'S ALLEGIANCE TO THE SUPREME COMMANDER!

The generals left the meeting politely, but many in that room were convinced they must get Hitler to change his mind. After hearing the plan, General Ludwig Beck, who had previously believed Hitler could restore Germany's honor and power, went much further. He eventually realized he could no longer serve this madman. The seeds of a plot to overthrow Hitler began to take root.

Despite being at the forefront of anti-Nazi resistance, Dietrich continued to be conflicted about what to do if he was called up to serve in the German army. He was certain he could never fire a bullet on behalf of the Nazis; but would he flee, or would he take the kind of stand that could cost him his life? He continually prayed, asking God to make the way clear.

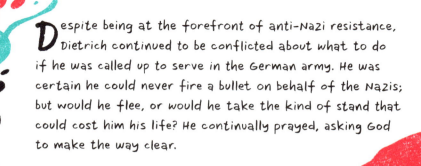

GOD, WHAT GOOD WOULD IT DO FOR ME TO BE SENT TO A GESTAPO PRISON, OR EXECUTED IN A PRISON CAMP?

But as his prayers piled up, God was silent.

If he fought for Germany, Dietrich would be betraying his beliefs. But on the other hand, if he deserted, his own family might be endangered. Dietrich needed a way out.

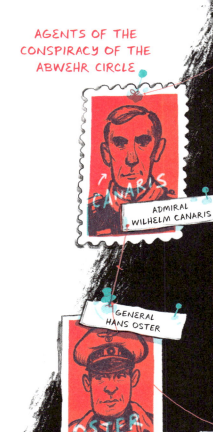

ADMIRAL
WILHELM CANARIS

GENERAL
HANS OSTER

It was around this time that Dietrich first became aware of the brewing conspiracy against Hitler. The information came through his brother-in-law Hans von Dohnányi, who worked for the Abwehr (pronounced UP-fair), the German spy agency. His mother's cousin General Paul von Hase (whom Dietrich called Uncle Paul), the military commander of Berlin, was also involved. Clearly, the spirit of rebellion was in Dietrich's blood.

Through these two, Dietrich was introduced to even higher operatives for the resistance. Could they provide a way out of his crisis, or perhaps even …

… a way out of Germany?

HANS VON DOHNÁNYI,
MARRIED TO DIETRICH'S
SISTER CHRISTINE

GENERAL PAUL VON HASE,
DIETRICH'S FIRST COUSIN
ONCE REMOVED

RÜDIGER SCHLEICHER,
MARRIED TO DIETRICH'S
SISTER URSULA

KLAUS BONHOEFFER,
DIETRICH'S BROTHER

THERE WERE MANY DIFFERENT CIRCLES OF CONSPIRACY AGAINST HITLER. THEY WORKED INDEPENDENTLY BUT GENERALLY WERE AWARE OF EACH OTHER.

•THE ABWEHR CIRCLE
•THE KREISAU CIRCLE
•THE GOERDELER CIRCLE
•THE FREIBURG CIRCLE

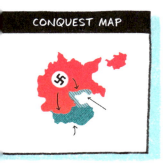

Just as he had promised, Hitler made good on his threats. In March 1938, he annexed Austria with nothing more than blustery speeches and the tactics of a schoolyard bully. The Austrian government was so terrified of war with a lunatic, they gladly gave Hitler their lunch money to prevent a fight. Emboldened by his easy triumph, Hitler set his sights on Austria's neighbor Czechoslovakia.

It is hard to explain why such bold aggression went so unchecked within the ranks of the German military, especially considering that many of the generals were disgusted with this kind of warmongering. But these men felt bound by an outdated sense of duty to their titles, ranks, and command structure. They feared publicly speaking out and being perceived as disloyal to Germany.

General Ludwig Beck, chief of the army general staff, resigned his position in protest of both Hitler's strategies and the other generals' passivity. Unlike some of his fellow officers, General Beck realized that obeying your commander was not the highest authority. A true leader had the duty to disregard orders if they were immoral. Just like Dietrich, General Beck found his DUTY TO GOD in conflict with his DUTY TO COUNTRY.

Even more important to understanding the generals' inaction was their total belief that Hitler could NOT sustain this high-wire act very long. Many in the army leadership believed that Hitler was completely unhinged and that his risky game of chicken with a new world war could only end in his disgraced exit from leadership.

They reasoned:

IF WE LET HITLER WALK THE PLANK ALONE, EVENTUALLY, HE WILL FALL TO THE SHARKS BELOW ON HIS OWN!

BUT THEY WERE WRONG.

Hitler conquered Austria without a single bullet ... AND GERMANY CHEERED! Hitler seized the Sudetenland in mountainous Czechoslovakia. This area, though in a different country, was home to many ethnic Germans. Hitler took it without a single tank shell ...

AND GERMANY CHEERED EVEN LOUDER!

Soon enough, the generals realized they had missed their chance to nudge him off the plank. Empowered by the rapturous adoration of the German people, Hitler now believed he could do anything to anyone.

It was in the midst of Hitler's seizure of Czechoslovakia that the Nazi war on Jews came out from the shadows and into the chilling moonlight. It began on November 9, 1938, with hours of remorseless terror that came to be known as "KRISTALLNACHT."

THE NIGHT OF

Earlier, in the first week of November 1938, a young Jewish boy shot and killed an official in the German embassy in Paris (the boy's father had been seized and deported by the Nazis). But this event, despite happening in another country, was all the Nazis needed as a pretense to release the nocturnal hounds.

Orders went out to every Gestapo station: terrorize the Jewish population.

Businesses were looted after the windows were smashed by SS and Gestapo agents. Synagogues were burned. Jews were beaten and killed in the street.

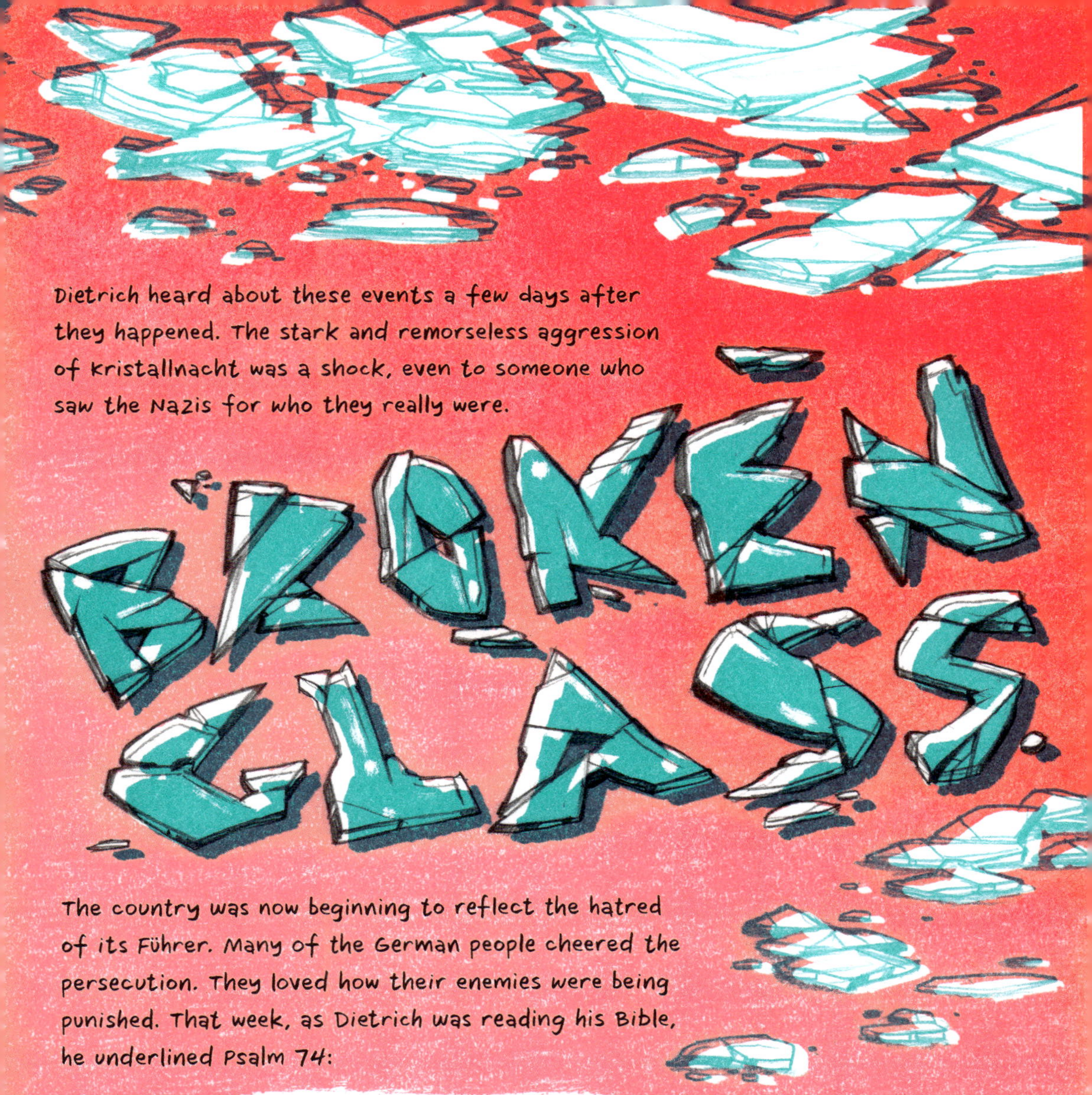

Dietrich heard about these events a few days after they happened. The stark and remorseless aggression of Kristallnacht was a shock, even to someone who saw the Nazis for who they really were.

BROKEN GLASS.

The country was now beginning to reflect the hatred of its Führer. Many of the German people cheered the persecution. They loved how their enemies were being punished. That week, as Dietrich was reading his Bible, he underlined Psalm 74:

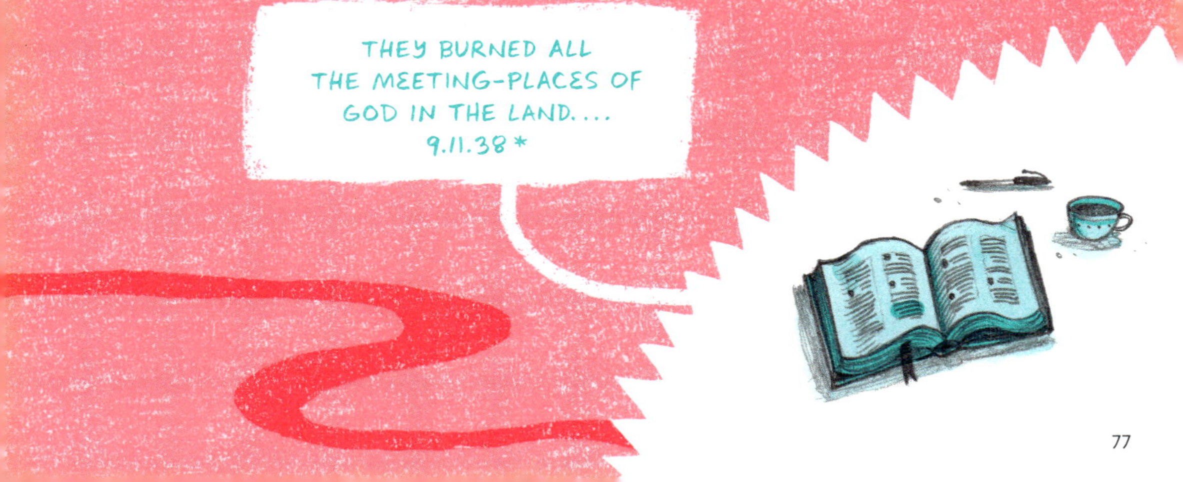
THEY BURNED ALL THE MEETING-PLACES OF GOD IN THE LAND....
9.11.38 *

Dietrich's resolve to resist Hitler had swelled into a holy anger. Christians must see the Jews as their brothers, as "children of the Covenant." He believed an attack on the Jewish people was an attack on all of God's children. IF THE CHURCH, IN THIS MOMENT, DID

NOT EXIST TO PROTECT THE OTHER,

IT HAD NO RIGHT TO BE CALLED THE CHURCH AT ALL.

As he closed his eyes, he could hear his Jewish heroes—King David, Elijah, Gideon, and the Apostle Paul— all crying out:

GOLIATH HAS RETURNED!

GOLIATH HAS RETURNED!

DIETRICH, IT IS YOUR TURN TO PICK UP THE SLING!

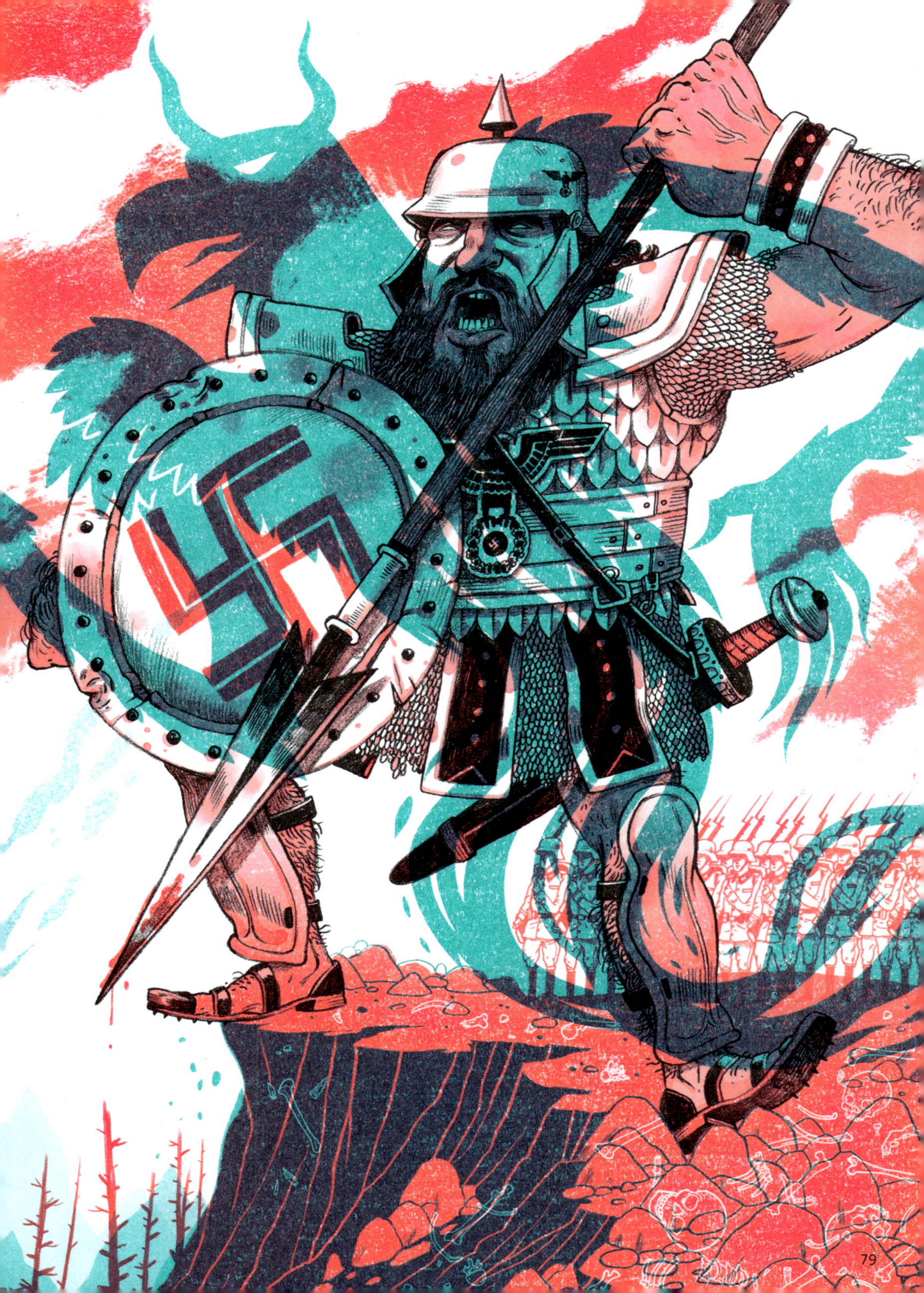

CONQUEST MAP

In January 1939, the Nazi government sent notice that all men born in 1906 (the year Dietrich was born) had to register for military service. The moment to decide whether to fight or not must come soon. War was dawning on the German horizon.

On January 30, 1939, just days after Dietrich got his draft notice, Hitler made his most audacious speech about the Jews yet. He called for the total annihilation of the Jewish people in all of Europe! All Jewish-owned stores were liquidated and the property seized by the government. It had become illegal to be a Jew in Germany.

BUT HITLER DIDN'T LIMIT HIS AGGRESSION TO THE JEWISH PEOPLE, HE WAS ESCALATING HIS WAR ON EUROPE AS WELL. NOT CONTENT WITH THE SMALL SECTION OF WESTERN CZECHOSLOVAKIA THAT HE HAD SEIZED IN THE FALL OF 1938, HITLER INVADED THE ENTIRE COUNTRY BY MARCHING ON THE CAPITAL, PRAGUE, IN MARCH 1939. BY DOING THIS, HITLER BLATANTLY DEFIED A PEACE TREATY HE HAD MADE WITH THE BRITISH IN THE FALL OF 1938. JUST A FEW MONTHS EARLIER, HITLER HAD PROMISED THE WORLD HE WOULD STOP CAUSING TROUBLE IF HE COULD KEEP HIS CLAIM TO THE SUDETENLAND AREA OF CZECHOSLOVAKIA. BRITAIN, WHICH WAS LEADING THESE "PEACE NEGOTIATIONS," GAVE IN TO HITLER'S DEMANDS, HOPING THAT AN "APPEASEMENT" WOULD SATISFY HITLER. IT DID NOT.

As Dietrich read the reports of Nazis marching down the streets of Prague, he knew that his time was running out. He could be forced into service any day now. In desperation, he decided to apply for a military deferment, for the allowed one-year term. That meant he wouldn't have to enlist until 1940. But where would he go? Dietrich's friends and colleagues in the remnants of the Confessing Church were eager to save him from the gears of the German war machine. After personal appeals to his connections in both England and America, he was granted a teaching position back in New York City. There he could minister to German refugees at Union Theological Seminary.

MAYBE FRANK WILL STILL BE THERE?

With great effort from his family connections inside the German government, and against all odds, Dietrich was cleared to leave Germany with a year-long deferral of military service. A miraculous last-minute escape had been made possible! He gave thanks to God beside his bed. God had opened a door to safety. On his knees, Dietrich searched for the Lord's will in a long and meandering prayer of thanks and praise. But, once again, his prayer came back empty. God was silent. Was it escape that the Lord really wanted for him?

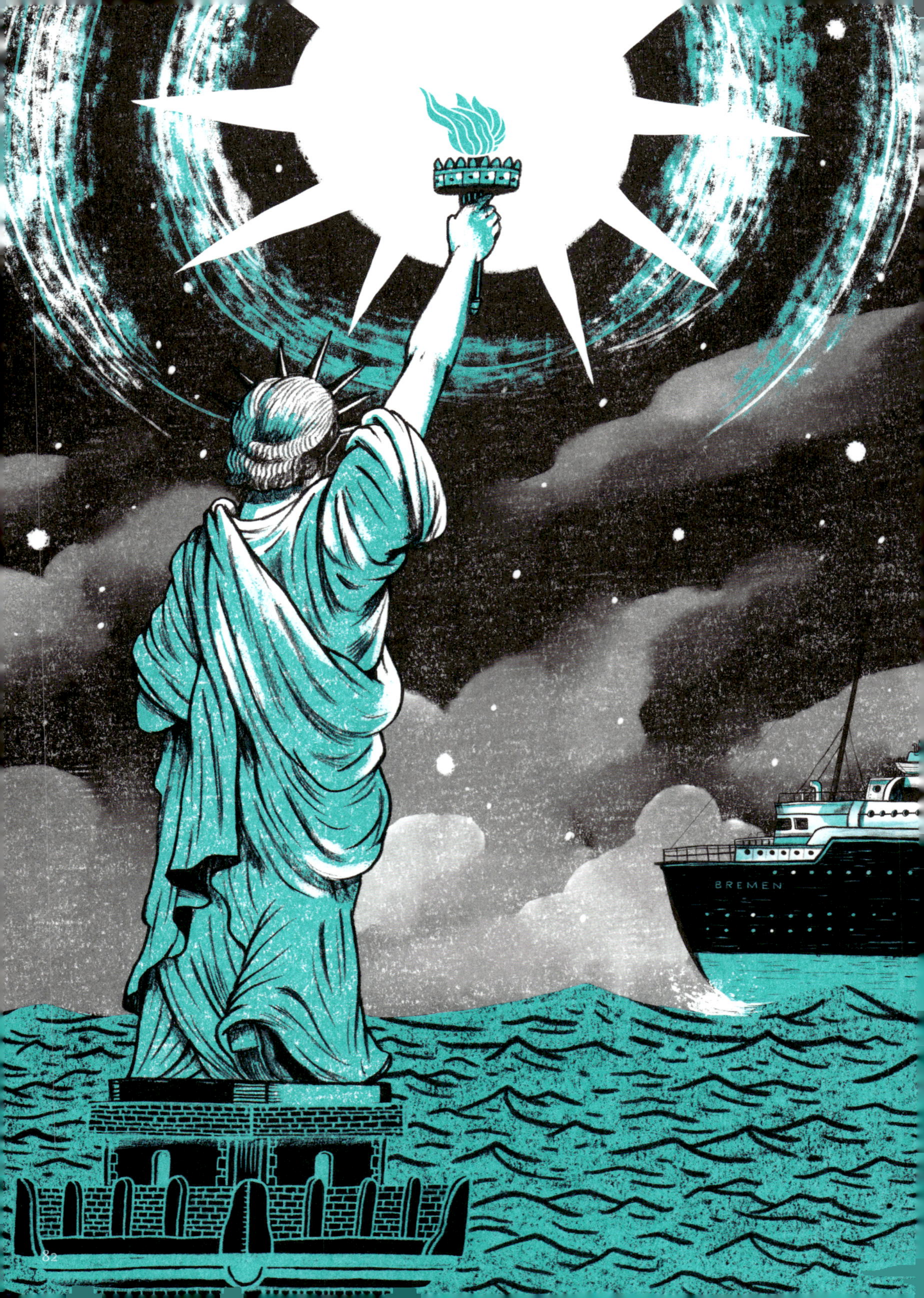
BREMEN

DIETRICH BOARDED
A SHIP IN JUNE 1939, BOUND
FOR AMERICA ONCE AGAIN. BUT THIS
TIME, EVERYTHING FELT DIFFERENT. THERE
WAS NO SENSE OF YOUTHFUL ADVENTURE. DIETRICH
WAS LEAVING BEHIND HIS FRIENDS, FAMILY, AND FELLOW
REBELS IN THE CONFESSING CHURCH. THEY WERE LEFT
TO FACE THE NAZIS WITHOUT HIM. HE KNEW IF WAR
DID BREAK OUT WHILE HE WAS IN NEW YORK, THERE
WOULD BE NO RETURN UNTIL THE BITTER END.

STANDING ON THE OCEAN LINER'S WINDY DECK AS
IT ENTERED NEW YORK HARBOR, HE GAZED UPON
THE STATUE OF LIBERTY. HE COULDN'T HELP
BUT FEEL UNSETTLED, EVEN A BIT ASHAMED.
LADY LIBERTY'S TORCH WAS HELD HIGH,
AND SHE STOOD UNBOWED AND
UNAFRAID ...
A LIGHT
IN THE
DARKNESS.

AM I AFRAID TO
LIVE AS SHE DOES?

THE CITY NO LONGER HELD ANY WONDER FOR HIM. IT FELT DARK AND COLD, LIKE A HIDING PLACE. NEVER BEFORE HAD HE FELT SO ADRIFT. HE WANDERED THE MONOTONE STREETS, A GHOST IN THE URBAN MIST. DIETRICH LONGED TO BE SOLID AND WHOLE AGAIN. HE WAS HOMESICK, EVEN FOR A SICKENED GERMANY. HE HAD ALWAYS BEEN A FAITHFUL LETTER WRITER, BUT NOW HIS LETTERS WERE NEARLY CONSTANT. DIETRICH POURED OUT HIS THOUGHTS AND FEARS IN A WATERFALL OF CORRESPONDENCE TO EBERHARD BETHGE.

"ALL I NEED IS GERMANY, THE BRETHREN. . . . I DO NOT UNDERSTAND WHY I AM HERE."*

EVERY NIGHT AND EVERY MORNING, HE PRAYED BY HIS BED IN THE MODEST QUARTERS GIVEN TO HIM BY THE SEMINARY. ONE SUCH MORNING, HE READ HIS BIBLE AND FOUND THIS PASSAGE IN ISAIAH 28:16:

"THE ONE WHO BELIEVES DOES NOT FLEE."

DIETRICH BELIEVED IN GOD. DIETRICH BELIEVED IN GERMANY. IT WAS AS IF THE LORD HAD LIT A CANDLE IN A DARK ROOM. HE SAW IT ALL SO CLEARLY NOW. HE KNEW HE MUST RETURN.

The more he thought about his life, the more he came to one simple conclusion: what he wanted more than anything was to be a part of Germany's future. Its past was long gone. Its present was in the hands of a demon wearing a red armband. If Dietrich had any right to the future of Germany, he had to be with it in the present, no matter the cost.

He packed his bags so quickly, the next resident of his room at the seminary found undone sheets, overturned chairs, and wads of paper covered with frantic German script everywhere. Dietrich knew it was a race against the first bullet being fired. He had to return to Germany as fast as possible. The war could start at any moment! Being stuck in America was not tolerable for Dietrich any longer. He wrote an apologetic letter to the British colleagues who had worked so hard to arrange his appointment at Union.

I KNOW WHICH OF THESE ALTERNATIVES I MUST CHOOSE, BUT I CANNOT MAKE THAT CHOICE IN SECURITY. ... I HAVE COME TO THE CONCLUSION THAT I HAVE MADE A MISTAKE IN COMING TO AMERICA.*

He left New York on July 7, 1939, leaving on one of the last boats to make the trans-Atlantic journey before the start of World War II. He had spent only 26 days in America. Dietrich had made his choice, and the choice was to risk it all: his safety, his career, his very life, all for the cause of justice in Germany.

Even though he had now shackled his future to Germany's, his sense of freedom had returned again. Dietrich's mind was focused and still. The quiet allowed him to pray again, to see the road ahead more clearly.

He asked the Lord for strength for the fight to come, and God drew near. Dietrich felt an abundance of peace as God's presence fell over him. He had no clear idea what he would do when he returned to his homeland. But as the New York skyline disappeared into the gray waves behind him, his thoughts began to linger on a single question:

WOULD GOD FORGIVE THE MURDERER OF A TYRANT?

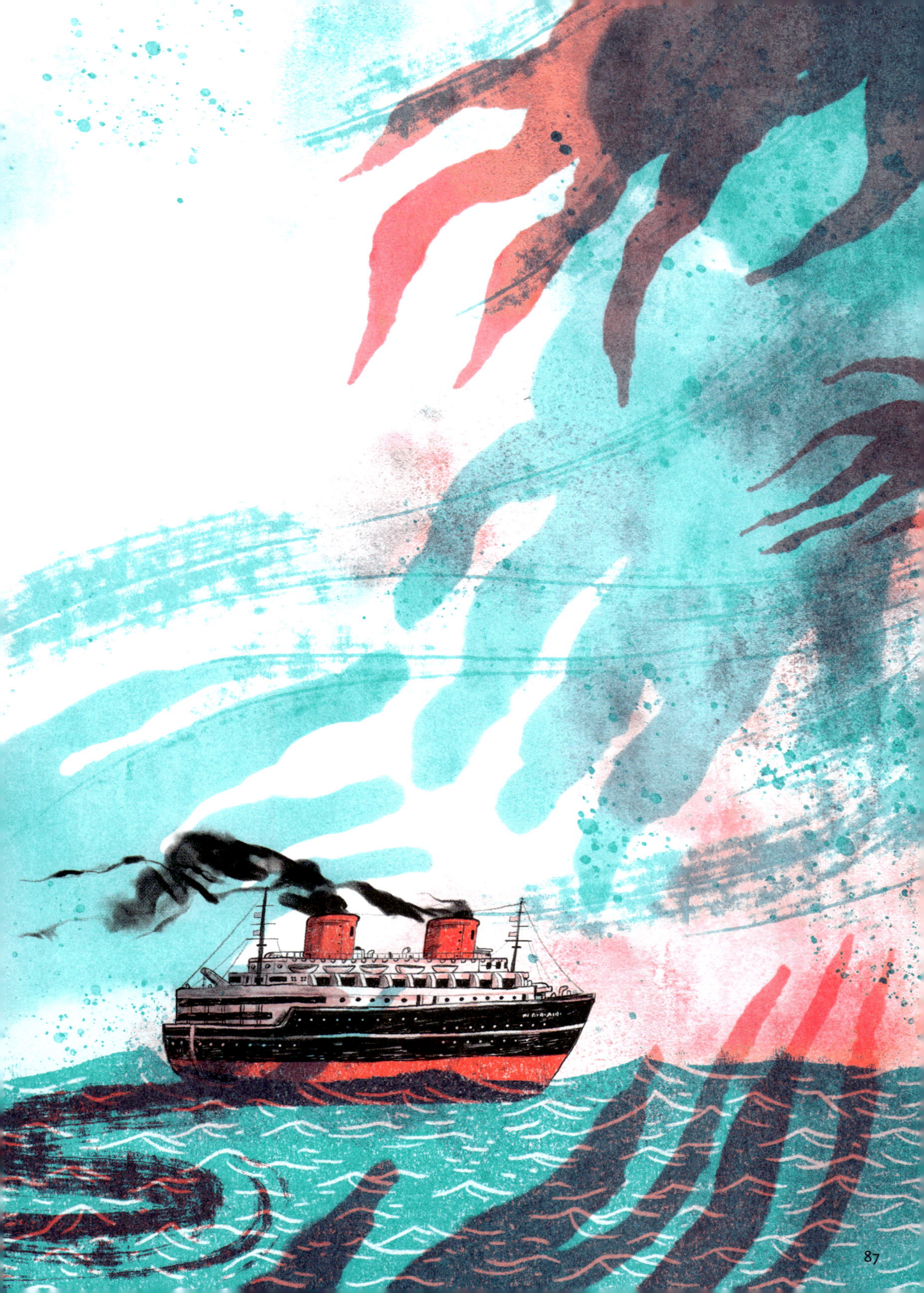

CHAPTER 5
JAMMING THE SPOKE

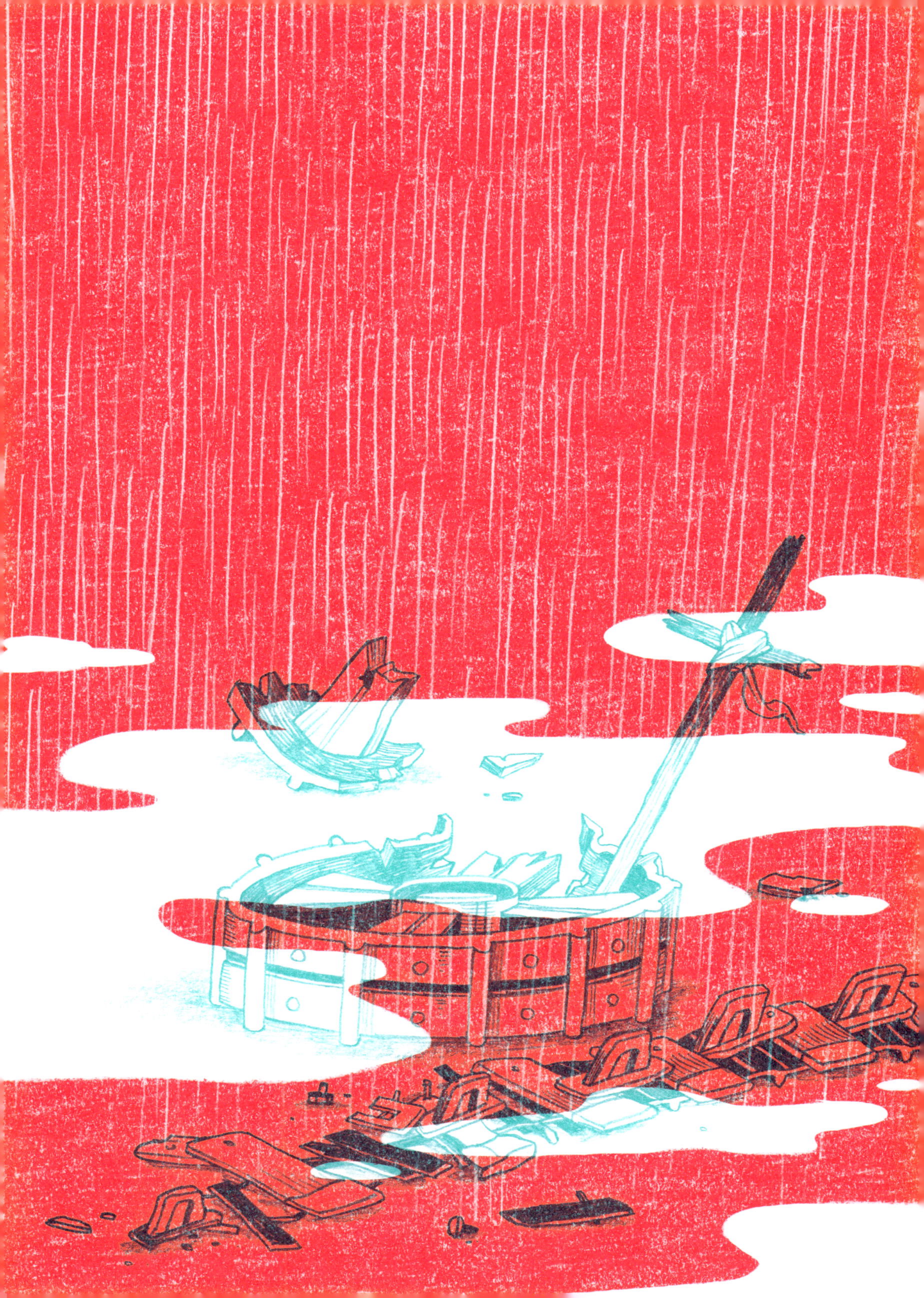

THE DANGERS OF RETURNING

to Germany confronted Dietrich before he even arrived back home. A fellow pastor in the Confessing Church, a bold preacher named Paul Schneider, was murdered in Buchenwald, a concentration camp. There were hundreds of these horrible sites appearing across the Reich. The Nazis called these detention camps KZ, short for KONZENTRATIONSLAGER. They functioned initially as work camps and prisons, but some would eventually become the efficient death factories used for Hitler's mass exterminations in the coming Holocaust.

Dietrich's year-long military deferral was quickly running out. He needed another option besides donning the German uniform or being shot for sedition. Dietrich was living inside a paradox. The more the horrors he saw inside Germany began to mount, the more he became convinced that the responsible action was the elimination of Hitler. But he served a gospel of peace. It seemed to him that both action and inaction produced a guilty responsibility.

Dietrich did his best to continue preaching, all the while aligning connections with the growing conspiracy to kill Hitler.

INACTION

ACTION

MANY OF THE NAZI CONCENTRATION CAMPS HAD SIGNS ON THE FRONT GATES THAT READ "ARBEIT MACHT FREI," WHICH MEANS "WORK SETS YOU FREE."

Dietrich, of course, knew of his brother Klaus's and his brother-in-law Hans Von Dohnányi's involvement in the Abwehr. They had been feeding information to Dietrich about the true nature of the Third Reich for years, but now Dietrich would become the spine of moral courage in the resistance.

WHO STANDS FAST?

ONLY THE MAN WHOSE FINAL STANDARD IS NOT
HIS REASON, HIS PRINCIPALS,
HIS CONSCIENCE, HIS FREEDOM,
OR HIS VIRTUE, BUT WHO IS READY TO SACRIFICE
ALL THIS WHEN HE IS CALLED TO OBEDIENT AND RESPONSIBLE

ACTION IN FAITH...

AND IN EXCLUSIVE ALLEGIANCE TO GOD.... WHERE ARE THESE

RESPONSIBLE PEOPLE?*

TO DIETRICH, THERE WAS NO DIFFERENCE BETWEEN AIDING THE CONSPIRACY AND PULLING THE TRIGGER HIMSELF.

I WOULD NOT HESITATE TO KILL THE MADMAN MYSELF! IF I SAW A LUNATIC PLOWING HIS CAR INTO THE CROWD, I COULD NOT CASUALLY STAND ON THE SIDEWALK AND SAY:

I AM A PASTOR. I'LL JUST WAIT TO BURY THE DEAD AFTERWARDS.*

DIETRICH, YOUR THREE WEEK TRAINING AT ULM RIFLE CLUB WAS A DISASTER.

Going forward, all of the conspirators would need Dietrich's holy confidence to continue their hard work. These brave men in the conspiracy were simultaneously betraying an oath to their country and their oath to God by planning the murder of their commander. As a kind of "chief pastor to the conspiracy," Dietrich used his gifts as both a writer and friend. The stakes and sorrows continued to mount for the resistance, but there was Dietrich. As a counselor and theologian, he would guide them through the thorns of regret and guilt.

His wisdom would chart a course into the moral unknown. Each of the conspirators needed to find a place where God would forgive them for plotting an assassination. Dietrich cherished this role, but he wondered: What more would he allow himself to do?

JUST A FEW WEEKS AFTER DIETRICH RETURNED FROM AMERICA, HITLER'S RAW HUNGER FOR CONQUEST GROWLED ONCE AGAIN.

Defying warnings from England and France to push no farther, Hitler illegally marched into Poland on September 1, 1939, without even an official declaration of war!

HITLER CLAIMED HE WAS ONLY INVADING BECAUSE THE POLISH ARMY HAD ATTACKED GERMAN TROOPS FIRST. BUT HITLER, LOOKING FOR AN EXCUSE TO START A WAR, HAD DRESSED UP HIS OWN MEN IN POLISH UNIFORMS AND HAD THEM "INVADE" A GERMAN RADIO STATION ON THE POLISH BORDER.

CONQUEST MAP

The year before, 1938, the British had merely warned him like a toddler on the verge of a tantrum. "NO MORE. Any more invading of countries and we're coming over there!" Hitler was certain the threats from England were paper tigers, nothing more than talk. But the Polish invasion had finally pushed England too far. Two days after Hitler invaded Poland, England and France felt they had no choice but to declare war on Germany.

WORLD WAR II HAD STARTED.

HITLER HAD TAKEN A BIG GAMBLE. HE HAD GUESSED THAT FRANCE AND BRITAIN WOULD THREATEN, BUT THEY WOULD NOT ACTUALLY FIGHT. THIS TIME HE LOST.

KNOWN AS A FALSE-FLAG OPERATION, IT LOOKED JUST LIKE A REAL ATTACK, BUT IT WAS ALL COMPLETELY STAGED!

MOST APPALLINGLY, HITLER DRESSED PRISONERS FROM CONCENTRATION CAMPS IN GERMAN UNIFORMS, KILLING SOME AND USING THEIR BODIES TO PROVE THE ATTACK ON GERMANY WAS REAL.

THIS HORRIBLE DECEIT WAS CALLED "OPERATION CANNED GOODS." (THAT IS HOW HITLER GROSSLY REFERRED TO PRISONERS HE KILLED TO USE AS PROPS.)

Shortly after the war broke out, Dietrich met the deputy chief of the Abwehr, General Hans Oster. This high commanding officer had joined the plot to end Hitler's reign. No one needed to convince Dietrich that Hitler was leading Germany to certain doom, but why were so many people connected to Hitler's own government joining the cause?

It all came from something Klaus and Hans had heard from General Oster. It was something horrible. They told Dietrich about unspeakable acts by the Nazi soldiers. Terrible things beyond the imagination were happening in Poland. Hitler's personal army, the SS, was committing such merciless acts of torture and terror that even seasoned army generals were reporting the crimes to their superiors with tears in their eyes.

The German war on Poland was swift and brutal. By the end of September, the capital, Warsaw, had fallen and the fighting was over. Poland was no more. Just like Czechoslovakia before it, the country was consumed into the German empire. Even Hitler's suspicions about the weak threats of the Allies turned out to be right. France and Britain had declared war but were not invading. They were debating what to do, while the Polish troops were being annihilated.

But, as if an instantaneous war on a peaceful neighbor weren't bad enough, the patchy reports coming back from the front lines were even worse. This is what Hans had heard:

DOHNÁNYI

The Waffen SS (a battlefield version of the SS—"Waffen" means "weapons") were not just fighting enemy soldiers; they were slaughtering the people of Poland. When the army captured a town or village, the SS would round up the Jews, the clergy, and the other citizens and kill them. This was not a war. This was an extermination!

In the honorable rules of war that the old army generals were trained to obey, women, children, and civilians—older men who were not in the army—were never killed! Even captured enemy soldiers, held as prisoners, were treated with respect. But in this horrible new world of Hitler's design, all people not of Aryan descent were deemed a disgrace to the new Third Reich. They were a liability and even called subhuman. Hitler had referred to his plan of domination in Poland as "housecleaning"—ridding the Reich of human filth by sweeping such people out of existence.

THE BRAZEN MURDER OF INNOCENT CIVILIANS TURNED EVEN THE MOST PATRIOTIC GENERALS TOWARD THE SIDE OF THE RESISTANCE. THEY BEGAN TO REALIZE IT WOULD NOT BE ENOUGH TO ARREST HITLER. THEY NOW BELIEVED HE MUST BE KILLED. AFTER THE DEATHLY HORRORS OF POLAND ...

A PLOT TO ASSASSINATE HITLER BECAME A REALITY.

When Dietrich heard of
these atrocities from
Hans and Klaus, he knew that
Germany had crossed a horrible
line. There would be no going back
to the Germany he had loved as a boy.
Hitler now ruled with the very powers
of hell. Mercy and justice were dethroned,
and in their place the Führer enshrined brutality,
revenge, and terror. The events in Poland were not a
fluke but an indication of the kind of savagery found
at the heart of the Nazi ideology.

There was no time to waste. Hitler would certainly not leave
his tanks idling. His engine of death was only fueled by chaos and
suffering. The conspirators knew they must act quickly, for each day
brought with it new terrors for the innocents. Who would be next?
The generals (well, some of them) were convinced that they must act.
Their fierce loyalties created intense factions, and soon the generals
squabbled over the details of how to move forward.

WHAT WILL HAPPEN
TO ALL THE NAZI
SUPPORTERS?

WHO WILL BE THE
NEW CHANCELLOR?

HOW SHOULD
WE DO IT?

WILL WE BE ABLE TO
GAIN THE CONFIDENCE
OF THE PEOPLE?

The days turned into weeks, and the passion behind the plan began
to falter. Some generals began to suggest again that Hitler would
undo himself on his own, and all they had to do was wait it out.
But the Nazi army did not tarry as the generals did. Hitler's army
marched on, and the great Nazi maw continued to swallow
entire countries in a single bite.

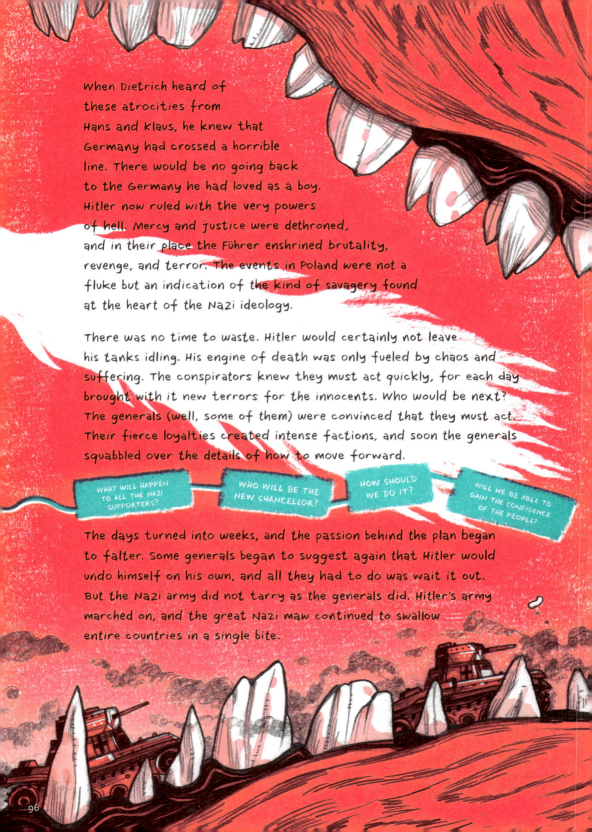

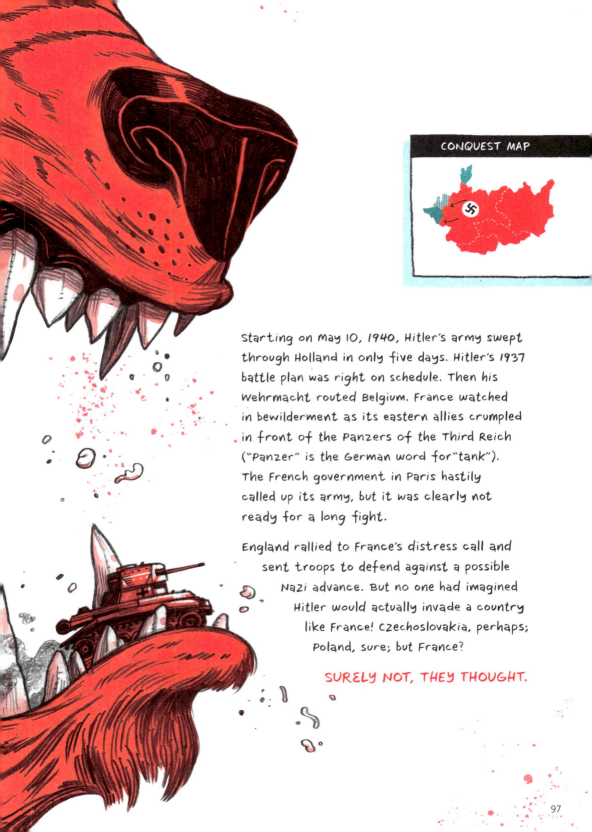

CONQUEST MAP

Starting on May 10, 1940, Hitler's army swept through Holland in only five days. Hitler's 1937 battle plan was right on schedule. Then his Wehrmacht routed Belgium. France watched in bewilderment as its eastern allies crumpled in front of the Panzers of the Third Reich ("Panzer" is the German word for "tank"). The French government in Paris hastily called up its army, but it was clearly not ready for a long fight.

England rallied to France's distress call and sent troops to defend against a possible Nazi advance. But no one had imagined Hitler would actually invade a country like France! Czechoslovakia, perhaps; Poland, sure; but France?

SURELY NOT, THEY THOUGHT.

1 When the Allied forces of British and French soldiers hastily prepared their defenses ...

2 They assumed that the Nazi attack would come along the same line the Germans had used in the first world war. The German army would slide north and attack through Belgium.

3 Indeed, Hitler had sent several divisions north into the Netherlands, but as a "feint," a false attack. Using this, Hitler drew the French into a clever trap.

THE GERMANY ARMY HAD DEVISED A BRILLIANT NEW WAY TO USE TANKS. THEY CALLED IT THE BLITZKRIEG, OR "LIGHTNING-WAR." IN THE FIRST WORLD WAR, THE TANKS WERE USED TO SUPPORT GROUND TROOPS. THE GROUND TROOPS WOULD MARCH IN FIRST, FOLLOWED BY THE SLOW AND CLUNKY TANKS TO HOLD THE GROUND GAINED. BUT THE NAZIS DID THE OPPOSITE: THEY BUILT NEW TANKS THAT WERE VERY FAST. THEN THEY PUT THEIR TANKS IN THE FRONT! THEY GROUPED THEM TOGETHER IN A WEDGE FORMATION AND PUNCHED THEM RIGHT THROUGH THE ENEMY'S FRONT LINES. IT WAS A BLISTERING ATTACK THAT LEFT THE ENEMY SOLDIERS AFRAID AND DISORGANIZED.

4 As the French chased the Germans north, the main force of Hitler's army went south and bored through the Ardennes Forest. The French had left it basically undefended. All the French generals agreed the Nazi army could never march through the densely wooded terrain of the Ardennes. They were wrong about Hitler again! Hitler rammed his 1,800 tanks through the forest in a single line and swept in behind the French, who were advancing toward the feint.

5 HITLER HAD CAUGHT THE FRENCH ARMY BETWEEN HIS TWO FORCES IN A CRUSHING PINCER. THE BRITISH, WITH THEIR BACKS AGAINST THE SEA, FLED HOME TO ENGLAND, AND THE FRENCH SURRENDERED. BY JUNE 14, NAZI TANKS ROLLED DOWN THE STREETS OF PARIS. IN LITTLE MORE THAN A MONTH, HITLER HAD CONQUERED THE MAJORITY OF WESTERN EUROPE.

HITLER VIEWED THE CAPTURE OF PARIS AS REVENGE FOR THE DESPISED TREATY OF VERSAILLES. HE ORCHESTRATED AN ODDLY PETTY MOMENT OF STAGECRAFT FOR THE SIGNING OF FRANCE'S SURRENDER AGREEMENT.

HE HAD THE SMALL RAILWAY CAR WHERE THE TREATY OF VERSAILLES WAS SIGNED IN 1919 TRANSPORTED TO PARIS FOR THE SPECIAL HUMILIATION OF THE FRENCH DIGNITARIES. HITLER WANTED THE SITE OF THEIR VICTORY OVER GERMANY IN WORLD WAR I TO BE THE VERY PLACE OF THEIR DEFEAT IN WORLD WAR II. (HE EVEN BROUGHT IN THE VERY SAME CHAIRS!) AFTERWARD, HITLER HAD HIS GOONS SOMEHOW HAUL THE ENTIRE RAILWAY CAR BACK TO BERLIN FOR A FUTURE MUSEUM OF HIS ACHIEVEMENTS.

THE GENERALS' SQUABBLING HAD COST THEM EVERYTHING.

Hitler had the one thing they had never thought possible: success! Many German people worshiped Hitler like a god. They heralded him as the new Napoleon: He was undefeated on the battlefield and destined by God to lead Germany into a new world order!

Even some of the generals began to change their minds. Doing the right thing was much harder with Germany on a winning streak! If they killed Hitler now, the people would surely revolt. He would become a martyr. Germany was gaining territory and resources, and all of Europe feared its power as never before. (Actually, the more they thought about it, the more the generals speculated they might get a promotion and a raise out of all this.)

Even the resistance in Dietrich's circle was stunned by the overwhelming victories on the battlefield. They had all assumed that Hitler would ruin Germany with foolhardy military bravado. The only outcome from such a blowhard leading Germany into war, they surmised, would be a crushing military defeat. But now they had to deal with colossal triumph!

Hitler's persona had swelled from a popular leader into a glowing idol of German supremacy. Even Zeus would have been jealous of his power and adoration. Riding this wave of popularity, his lust for domination swelled with each passing day. And just who would be next? The Third Reich set out to conquer the unconquered: Britain.

Throwing the British forces back into the sea had been a great victory. However, Hitler was not just raising the stakes but betting the whole house. How could Hitler get all his men across the sea and also hold the ground they had already claimed in France? Hitler's answer came from his toad-like yes-man, Air Marshal Hermann Göring: The Luftwaffe would win the battle in the skies! The generals said Hitler's plan was suicide. But, brushing aside his commanders' concerns as mere "defeatism," Hitler began his air war. German planes began daily bombings of British airfields and radar installations all along the British coast. Next came "the Blitz," a series of bone-chilling nighttime bombings of London's civilians in September 1940. Hitler's plan was to soften the English underbelly for his massive surface invasion across the English Channel. He called it (rather literally) Operation Sea Lion.

The plans for the removal of Hitler had become ten, perhaps a hundred, times more difficult. There would be no quick solution with so much power and success in the office of the Führer. The conspiracy would have to dig in for a long winter.

CONQUEST MAP

THE BLITZ OF LONDON

IN JULY 1940, DIETRICH WAS PREACHING TO A SMALL GROUP OF PEOPLE WHEN THE GESTAPO STORMED IN AND BROKE UP THE MEETING.

SOMEHOW, DIETRICH WAS ABLE TO ESCAPE ARREST—BUT HE REALIZED THAT HIS ABILITY TO PREACH TO THE REBELLIOUS CHURCH WAS FINALLY OVER. THE GESTAPO WAS CLEARLY TRACKING HIM. EVEN HIS RELATIVELY FREE MOVEMENT AROUND THE COUNTRY WOULD BE AT RISK. DIETRICH DECIDED TO ABANDON HIS PUBLIC PREACHING AND OFFICIALLY JOIN THE CONSPIRACY.

THROUGH HIS CONNECTIONS WITH OSTER AND HIS BROTHER-IN-LAW HANS, DIETRICH AGREED TO BECOME A V-MANN (A SPY) FOR THE ABWEHR.

CANARIS

ADMIRAL WILHELM CANARIS WAS THE ABWEHR STATION CHIEF AND A MAJOR FIGURE IN THE MILITARY. HE HAD JOINED THE CONSPIRACY AFTER THE ATROCITIES IN POLAND. UNDER CANARIS, DIETRICH WOULD NOT BE A NORMAL SPY—HE WOULD JOIN THE AGENCY AS A DOUBLE AGENT SPYING ON HIS HOME COUNTRY. TO THE NAZI GOVERNMENT, HE WOULD APPEAR TO BE A LOYAL AGENT, WORKING TO GAIN SECRETS ABROAD FOR THE THIRD REICH, IN THE GUISE OF A MERE PASTOR.

IN REALITY, HE WOULD BE JUST THE OPPOSITE, A RESISTANCE SPY UNDER COVER AS A NAZI PASTOR, TRYING TO SMUGGLE INFORMATION TO THE ALLIES ABOUT HOW TO DEFEAT GERMANY AND HITLER HIMSELF.

DIETRICH'S APPOINTMENT TO THE ABWEHR SOLVED MANY OF HIS PRESSING PROBLEMS, BUT ALSO CREATED NEW ONES. STILL, JOINING THE SPY AGENCY IMMEDIATELY TOOK HIM OUT OF THE CROSSHAIRS OF THE GESTAPO.

BOTH THE ABWEHR AND THE GESTAPO WERE SPYING FOR HITLER, BUT THEY WERE BITTER RIVALS. LUCKILY, THE ABWEHR HELD THE TRUMP CARD OVER THE GESTAPO IN THE COMMAND STRUCTURE. THIS MEANT THAT BECAUSE HE WAS ONE OF THE ABWEHR'S AGENTS, THE GESTAPO HAD TO LEAVE DIETRICH ALONE! THIS ALSO GAVE DIETRICH THE DIPLOMATIC PAPERS TO TRAVEL ABROAD.

DIETRICH COULDN'T TELL ANYONE HIS DANGEROUS SECRET.

EVEN HIS FRIENDS IN THE CONFESSING CHURCH NOT CONNECTED DIRECTLY TO THE CONSPIRACY COULDN'T KNOW ANYTHING ABOUT HIS MISSION. THIS MADE FOR MANY AWKWARD CONVERSATIONS WHEN DIETRICH REVEALED HE WAS NOW WORKING FOR THE NAZIS. MANY OF HIS FRIENDS COULDN'T UNDERSTAND WHAT HAD HAPPENED THAT WOULD MAKE THEIR BELOVED DIETRICH WORK FOR THE ENEMY! HOW DIETRICH LONGED TO TELL THEM THE TRUTH ...

BUT HE HAD TO PROTECT THE CONSPIRACY AT ALL COSTS.

SIN BOLDLY

IS THIS WHAT LUTHER MEANT WHEN HE SAID THAT CHRISTIANS SHOULD "SIN BOLDLY"? ARE THERE MOMENTS IN HISTORY WHEN ETHICAL PEOPLE MUST TAKE EXTREME ACTIONS, EVEN IF THOSE ARE AGAINST THEIR MORAL CODE?

HIS LORD COMMANDED HIM TO NEVER BEAR FALSE WITNESS, BUT NOW HE MUST LIE.

HIS LORD COMMANDED NOT TO KILL, BUT NOW HE WAS INVOLVED IN PLOTTING A MURDER.

THERE WERE WRONG CHOICES IN EVERY DIRECTION. IT SEEMED HE MUST SIN AND HOPE GOD WOULD FORGIVE HIM.

DECEPTION WAS NOW PART OF HIS ACT OF FAITH.

EVEN A MONTH BEFORE DIETRICH JOINED THE ABWEHR, EBERHARD NOTICED THAT DIETRICH WAS ALREADY BEGINNING TO ACT THE PART. ON ONE OCCASION DURING THE FRENCH INVASION IN JUNE, DIETRICH AND EBERHARD WERE HAVING LUNCH AT AN OUTDOOR CAFÉ NEAR FINKENWALDE, WHEN OVER THE LOUDSPEAKER, THERE CAME THE STATE ANNOUNCEMENT:

"FRANCE HAS FALLEN. GERMANY HAS TRIUMPHED!"

HEIL HITLER!

DIETRICH SHOT OUT OF HIS SEAT AND THREW HIS HAND OUT IN THE HITLER SALUTE, SHOUTING, "HEIL HITLER!" ALONG WITH THE REST OF THE CAFÉ.

DIETRICH, WHY ARE YOU DOING THIS?

ARE YOU CRAZY? RAISE YOUR ARM!

WE SHALL HAVE TO RUN RISKS FOR VERY DIFFERENT THINGS NOW, BUT NOT FOR THAT SALUTE!*

His first major assignment from Admiral Canaris was small but essential.

DIETRICH, YOU MUST FIND US SUPPORT FOR THE ASSASSINATION. WE WILL NEVER SURVIVE WITHOUT ASSURANCES FROM THE WEST.

He was tasked with using his contacts in churches abroad as cover and approaching agents of foreign governments at war with Germany—and convincing them of the impossible: that there were still good people in Germany, trying to end the war from the inside.

Killing Hitler was not as easy as just pulling the trigger. The conspirators also wanted to save Germany from the fate it had suffered at the end of World War I. The Allies had to know that the conspiracy existed and that it was on the side of justice. Once Hitler and his inner circle were dead, the new government would need the Allies to help fight off the remnants of the Nazis—otherwise an ensuing internal power struggle would cripple Germany's recovery.

Dietrich's was a very difficult assignment. In wartime, there is no way to communicate with sympathetic agents of the foreign governments you are fighting, unless you send a messenger. But that messenger might be a spy himself. Why would the foreign governments trust you? The messenger could be arrested or shot on the spot! The conspiracy thought that Dietrich, as a pastor, might be able to deliver such a delicate message with less suspicion.

DIETRICH HAD TO SOMEHOW GET THE MISSION OF THE CONSPIRACY IN FRONT OF BRITAIN'S PRIME MINISTER, WINSTON CHURCHILL, HIMSELF.

CHURCHILL

Hitler's plans to invade England floundered. Even Hitler realized the difficulty of a full-scale invasion across the open water of the English Channel. Plus the British Air Force had inflicted much heavier losses on the German Luftwaffe than expected (despite Göring's ill-founded assurances otherwise). So Hitler turned east to find a new people to conquer for the moment. Meeting with his generals once again, he casually announced the next target of the German attack: Soviet Russia.

THE ARMY GENERALS WERE RUNNING OUT OF WAYS TO BE HORRIFIED.

Hitler had actually made a peace treaty with the leader of Russia, Joseph Stalin, just two years earlier. Clearly, treaties and promises meant nothing to Hitler. He was convinced God had appointed him as savior, so he believed no choice he made could possibly fail.

CONQUEST MAP

On the Führer's orders, the German Wehrmacht invaded Russia in June 1941. Hitler's command to the army generals on the battlefield: No mercy. They must execute captured Russian officers. Hitler demanded the unthinkable from his generals: the killing of prisoners! Many captured Russian infantry soldiers were held without food and died of starvation in captivity.

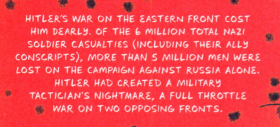

HITLER'S WAR ON THE EASTERN FRONT COST HIM DEARLY. OF THE 6 MILLION TOTAL NAZI SOLDIER CASUALTIES (INCLUDING THEIR ALLY CONSCRIPTS), MORE THAN 5 MILLION MEN WERE LOST ON THE CAMPAIGN AGAINST RUSSIA ALONE. HITLER HAD CREATED A MILITARY TACTICIAN'S NIGHTMARE, A FULL THROTTLE WAR ON TWO OPPOSING FRONTS.

But by December 1941, Hitler's streak of victories finally ran aground. Hitler had underestimated the massive resources of the Russians. A bitter Russian winter froze the German men and their equipment, and the army was overwhelmed by millions of Russian troops and thousands of Russian tanks. Hitler blamed the new phenomenon of failures on his generals' rampant attitude of "defeatism." In a raging fury, Hitler assumed personal command of the entire army, removing the generals' authority on the battlefield!

THE UNITED STATES OF AMERICA ENTERS WORLD WAR II

ON DECEMBER 7, 1941, THE JAPANESE LAUNCHED A SURPRISE ATTACK ON THE AMERICAN NAVAL BASE IN PEARL HARBOR, HAWAII. JAPAN WAS A GERMAN ALLY, AND WHEN HITLER HEARD OF THE ATTACK, HE FOOLISHLY DECLARED WAR ON AMERICA AS WELL. THIS LED PRESIDENT FRANKLIN D. ROOSEVELT TO DECLARE WAR ON BOTH JAPAN AND GERMANY. AS HE HAD WITH RUSSIA, HITLER HAD NEEDLESSLY ADDED ANOTHER FORMIDABLE FOE TO GERMANY'S ENEMY LIST.

r'skov

Kalini (Tver)

Moscow

Vitebsk

olensl

rorisov

o Mogilev

o Tula

Riazan

sk

o Orel

iamb

U N I O N O F

o Voronezh

o Kursk

c Satauov

During this time, Dietrich began his role of spying for the Nazis in name, but secretly working against them. Operating as a double agent, he traveled outside of Germany, talking to churches and ambassadors, covertly trying to gather foreign support for the assassination attempt. In September 1941, he returned to Germany and saw something new. All the Jews were forced to wear yellow star badges on their clothes, identifying them as Jews. Dietrich feared the worst for his Jewish friends and family members (fortunately, his twin sister, Sabine, who had married into a Jewish family, had been evacuated to England with her husband and daughters several years before).

When Dietrich spoke with his friends abroad, he felt that the situation had become almost hopeless in Germany. He said,

"IF YOU WANT TO KNOW THE TRUTH, I PRAY FOR THE DEFEAT OF MY NATION. FOR I BELIEVE THAT IS THE ONLY WAY TO PAY FOR ALL THE SUFFERING WHICH MY COUNTRY HAS CAUSED IN THE WORLD."*

At this low point, Dietrich was tasked with a weighty assignment, "Operation 7." The Abwehr conspirators would be smuggling seven endangered Jews and people of Jewish descent out of Germany. Dietrich's brother-in-law Hans had designed a plan to evacuate this small group of Jews to Switzerland under the protective cover of the Abwehr.

With the news of mass Jewish deportations to the dreaded concentration camps, they had to act quickly!

The plan was complex and involved intense planning, but Dietrich was eager to be a part of it. The operation involved more trickery. Hans would convince the Nazi SS chief, Heinrich Himmler, and the government watchers that these Jews were to become Abwehr agents so they could travel to other countries and tell foreign leaders the Jews were being treated well by Germany. Of course, the gambit was that they were going to do the exact opposite, and would never return to Germany.

The problem was finding people in the foreign countries who wanted to harbor the escaping Jews. Dietrich's friends began to worry that if they didn't get these people out soon, they would be rounded up and shipped to concentration camps. Dietrich traveled abroad to find travel visas and sponsors for the escapees before they arrived. Getting a country to harbor Jewish refugees was very difficult, and he relied on the support of leaders he knew in the church. He wrote passionate letters to his friends in the Swiss church for help.

IN THE FIRST FEW WEEKS OF OCTOBER 1941, 60,000 JEWS FROM BERLIN ALONE WERE TRANSPORTED TO CONCENTRATION CAMPS. THIS WAS THE VERY BEGINNING OF ONE OF THE MOST ATROCIOUS ACTS OF GENOCIDE EVER: THE HOLOCAUST.

AT A MEETING IN JANUARY 1942, GERMAN OFFICER REINHARD HEYDRICH CALMLY PROPOSED TO HITLER THE "FINAL SOLUTION OF THE JEWISH QUESTION": TOTAL ELIMINATION. GAS CHAMBERS DESIGNED FOR EFFICIENT MASS KILLINGS WERE QUIETLY CONSTRUCTED IN CONCENTRATION CAMPS ACROSS NAZI-OCCUPIED EUROPE.

DIETRICH AND HIS FRIENDS, EVEN WITH THEIR VALUABLE CONNECTIONS INSIDE GERMAN INTELLIGENCE, KNEW ONLY PART OF THE WHOLE STORY.

One of Dietrich's letters finally broke the impasse. After much negotiation, the Swiss government agreed to allow in the refugees! But they agreed only on a big condition: They needed a large amount of money for their trouble. Frustrated but grateful, Dietrich, Hans, and the other Abwehr spies had to secretly secure the currency. Plus the original group of seven had now swelled to fourteen! At the end of September 1941, after a frantic escape, all fourteen refugees finally made it out of Germany.

BUT THE VICTORY CAME AT HIGH COST. THE HASTE WITH WHICH THE ABWEHR SPIES REQUESTED THE MONEY MADE SOME IN THE GESTAPO SUSPICIOUS. THE GESTAPO, WHO HATED THE ABWEHR, NOTICED THE LARGE TRANSFER OF MONEY AND BEGAN AN INVESTIGATION. EVERYONE INVOLVED IN OPERATION 7 WAS SUDDENLY UNDER DEEP SUSPICION FOR SOME KIND OF EMBEZZLEMENT. THE SPIES TOOK CAREFUL STEPS TO MAKE SURE THEIR TREACHERY WASN'T DISCOVERED, HOPING THE TRAIL WOULD GROW COLD. BUT ONE SUCCESS WAS NOT ENOUGH FOR HANS AND DIETRICH. THEY WANTED TO PLOT MANY MORE RESCUE OPERATIONS. THERE WERE SO MANY PEOPLE TO SAVE!

Next, Hans was given a special task by General Canaris. He was to carefully document the Nazi atrocities. They dubbed it the "Chronicles of Shame" but later called it the Zossen Files to cloak its true purpose. They compiled detailed records of the killings in Poland and the crimes against the Jews. The conspirators knew they needed a way to show the German people that Hitler was downright evil and, ultimately, that his assassination was justified. But this file was extremely dangerous. It proved the conspiracy existed down to the smallest detail. If the Gestapo ever found the file, it would be a disaster for everyone. Hans, Klaus, Dietrich, Canaris, and Oster could be executed for treason.

Despite the danger, Dietrich carried on. In May 1942, he traveled to Geneva, Switzerland, and learned from his covert contacts that his English friend Bishop Bell would be in Sweden for three weeks. This sort of information was nearly impossible to get in Germany during the war. Under the cover of being a Nazi agent to monitor a church conference, Dietrich left for Sweden. This would represent the conspiracy's best chance to get word directly to the British high command. Once they finally met, Dietrich confessed his secret to the Bishop. He was a spy, and he was part of the resistance against Hitler.

MY LORD BISHOP, CAN YOU PASS A MESSAGE ALONG TO WINSTON CHURCHILL ABOUT THE GERMAN RESISTANCE? IT IS OUR MOST DESPERATE HOUR. WE NEED THE SUPPORT OF THE ALLIES.

DIETRICH, YOU KNOW THAT I BELIEVE YOU. BUT IMAGINE YOU ARE IN CHURCHILL'S SHOES. WHY SHOULD HE BELIEVE, LET ALONE ACT, ON ANYTHING FROM A GERMAN?

GERMANS ARE WILLING TO SUFFER FOR OUR SINS, BISHOP. WE DO NOT WISH TO ESCAPE JUDGMENT.

I CAN DELIVER THE MESSAGE, DIETRICH. BUT DON'T GET YOUR HOPES UP. CHURCHILL IS IN NO MOOD TO SOFTEN HIS RESOLVE TOWARD HITLER.

NEITHER ARE WE!

Bishop Bell was good on his word. When he arrived back in London, he sent a letter to Anthony Eden, the British Foreign Minister. But the message landed with a thud. From the point of view of Churchill and the Allied high command, there was nothing acceptable but total defeat of Germany and unconditional surrender. Why should they let a pastor talking about a "phantom conspiracy" change their battle plans? The fact that Dietrich's most successful spy mission was a complete failure, though he never knew it, is proof of what long odds the conspiracy faced.

Meanwhile, the Gestapo wasn't giving up. Despite the conspirators' best attempts to throw them off, the Gestapo was hot on the trail of that suspicious transfer of currency that had saved the day for Operation 7. The network of Abwehr spies were now racing against a Gestapo embezzlement investigation. They must get to Hitler, and soon.

MARIA ↘

Dietrich Bonhoeffer's life was constantly tormented with bad timing. Just as the conspiracy against Hitler was building momentum toward an attack, Dietrich was thrown a beautiful complication. Her name was Maria von Wedemeyer.

She was the granddaughter of Ruth von Kleist-Retzow, one of the earliest supporters of his rebel seminary at Finkenwalde. When they first met, what seemed like a lifetime ago, Maria was twelve. Dietrich had hardly given her a second thought since then. But in August 1943, Maria's father was killed fighting the Russian army on the eastern front. Ruth asked her old friend Dietrich if he would come to do the service.

Since the rise of the Third Reich, Dietrich had decided that marriage was probably not a real possibility for him. In a world so full of risk and uncertainty, how could he consider the idea of falling in love? But that all changed when he saw Maria again.

NOW SHE WAS A GROWN WOMAN, BRAVE, CONFIDENT, AND BEAUTIFUL.

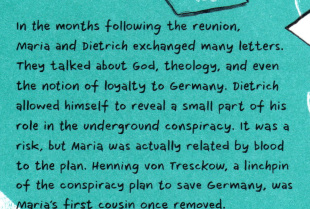

In the months following the reunion, Maria and Dietrich exchanged many letters. They talked about God, theology, and even the notion of loyalty to Germany. Dietrich allowed himself to reveal a small part of his role in the underground conspiracy. It was a risk, but Maria was actually related by blood to the plan. Henning von Tresckow, a linchpin of the conspiracy plan to save Germany, was Maria's first cousin once removed.

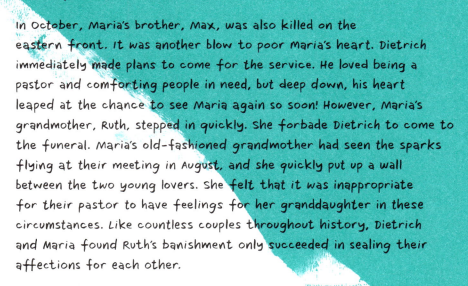

In October, Maria's brother, Max, was also killed on the eastern front. It was another blow to poor Maria's heart. Dietrich immediately made plans to come for the service. He loved being a pastor and comforting people in need, but deep down, his heart leaped at the chance to see Maria again so soon! However, Maria's grandmother, Ruth, stepped in quickly. She forbade Dietrich to come to the funeral. Maria's old-fashioned grandmother had seen the sparks flying at their meeting in August, and she quickly put up a wall between the two young lovers. She felt that it was inappropriate for their pastor to have feelings for her granddaughter in these circumstances. Like countless couples throughout history, Dietrich and Maria found Ruth's banishment only succeeded in sealing their affections for each other.

The crisis in Germany had made everything in Dietrich's life feel temporary and fragile. He so often longed for something solid, a tether of hope to the future. It was completely irrational to make plans and fall in love when the world was on fire. His feelings for young Maria were so small when set next to the scene unfolding around him.

yet, here he was, falling in love.
He wrote this to Maria ... asking her to marry him.

"I WANT TO CARE FOR YOU AND ALLOW THE DAWNING OF JOY OF OUR LIFE TO MAKE YOU LIGHT AND HAPPY. ... I UNDERSTAND AND UNDERSTOOD ALSO THROUGHOUT THESE PAST WEEKS—IF NOT ENTIRELY WITHOUT PAIN—THAT FOR YOU IT CANNOT BE EASY TO SAY YES TO ME, AND I WILL NEVER FORGET THAT. AND IT IS THIS, YOUR YES, WHICH ALONE CAN GIVE ME THE COURAGE AS WELL NO LONGER TO SAY ONLY NO TO MYSELF. SAY NO MORE ABOUT THE 'FALSE IMAGE' I COULD HAVE OF YOU. I WANT NO 'IMAGE'; I WANT YOU, JUST AS I BEG YOU WITH MY WHOLE HEART TO WANT NOT AN IMAGE OF ME BUT ME MYSELF; AND YOU MUST KNOW THOSE ARE TWO DIFFERENT THINGS. ... LET US TAKE EACH OTHER AS WE ARE—WITH THANKS AND BOUNDLESS TRUST IN GOD, WHO HAS LED US TO THIS POINT AND NOW LOVES US."*

Much came to light, both big and small, in January 1943. Dietrich and Maria announced their engagement, and the plan for the long-awaited assassination attempt was finalized. The plot was code-named ...

OPERATION FLASH

It would strike Hitler as he traveled back from a visit to the eastern war front. The plan was a simple concept: plant a bomb on Hitler's plane with a delayed fuse to explode while it was in the air. The event would look like an accident and help defuse the political fallout that would come with brazen public assassination.

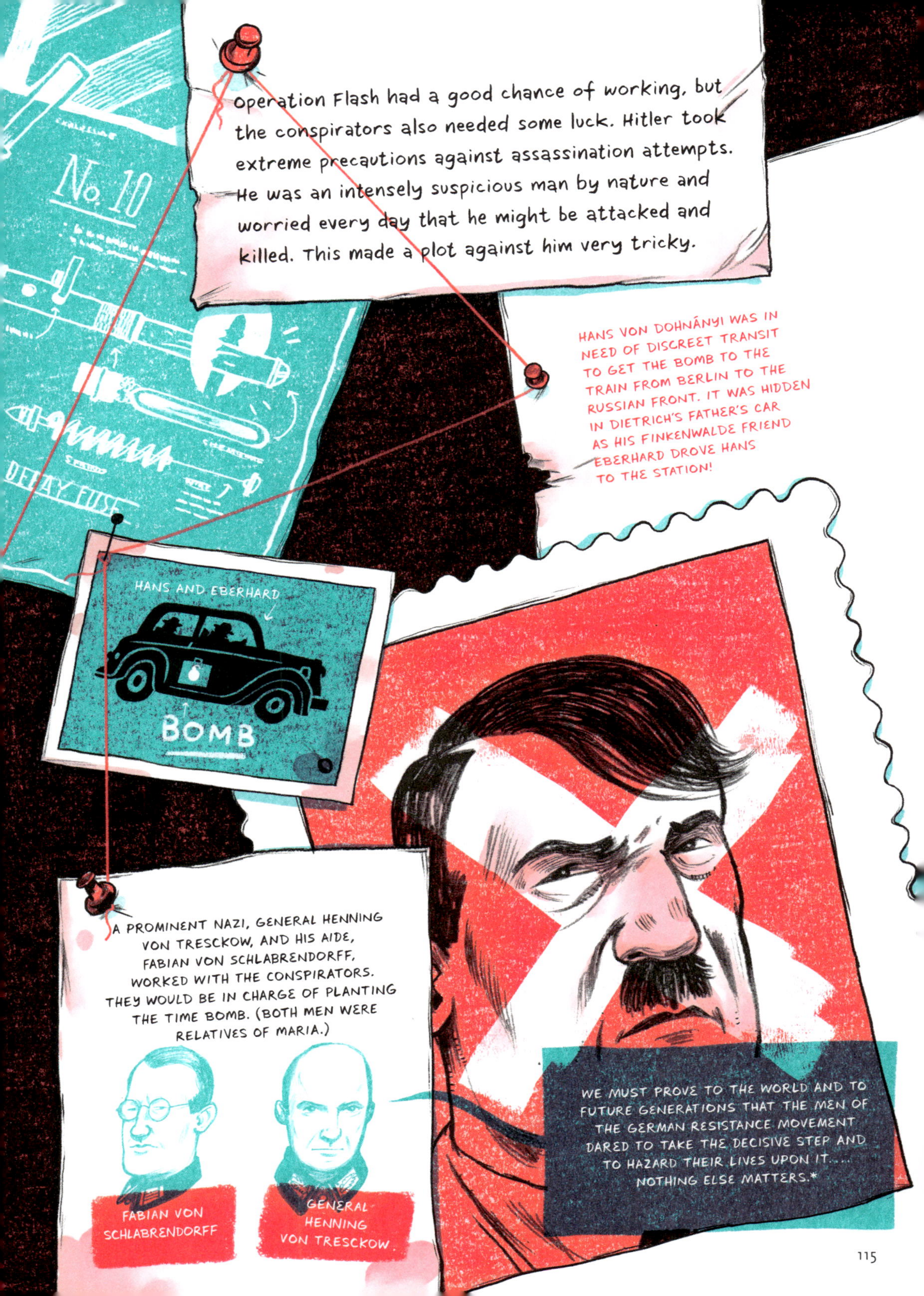
Operation Flash had a good chance of working, but the conspirators also needed some luck. Hitler took extreme precautions against assassination attempts. He was an intensely suspicious man by nature and worried every day that he might be attacked and killed. This made a plot against him very tricky.
No. 10
DELAY FUSE
HANS VON DOHNÁNYI WAS IN NEED OF DISCREET TRANSIT TO GET THE BOMB TO THE TRAIN FROM BERLIN TO THE RUSSIAN FRONT. IT WAS HIDDEN IN DIETRICH'S FATHER'S CAR AS HIS FINKENWALDE FRIEND EBERHARD DROVE HANS TO THE STATION!
HANS AND EBERHARD
BOMB
A PROMINENT NAZI, GENERAL HENNING VON TRESCKOW, AND HIS AIDE, FABIAN VON SCHLABRENDORFF, WORKED WITH THE CONSPIRATORS. THEY WOULD BE IN CHARGE OF PLANTING THE TIME BOMB. (BOTH MEN WERE RELATIVES OF MARIA.)
FABIAN VON SCHLABRENDORFF
GENERAL HENNING VON TRESCKOW
WE MUST PROVE TO THE WORLD AND TO FUTURE GENERATIONS THAT THE MEN OF THE GERMAN RESISTANCE MOVEMENT DARED TO TAKE THE DECISIVE STEP AND TO HAZARD THEIR LIVES UPON IT.... NOTHING ELSE MATTERS.*

THE ENGLISH-MADE BOMB DIDN'T HAVE ANY TICKING PARTS, SO IT WOULDN'T BE NOTICED. THE FUSE WAS FULL OF ACID THAT WOULD EAT AWAY AT A TINY WIRE THAT HELD THE FIRING PIN. ONLY THE ABWEHR WOULD HAVE HAD ACCESS TO THIS KIND OF BOMB. IF THE BOMB WAS DISCOVERED, EVERYONE INSIDE THE SPY AGENCY WOULD BE IMPLICATED.

The attempt took place the evening of March 13, 1943. Tresckow and Schlabrendorff were called to dine with the Führer before an evening flight. During the meal, General Tresckow leaned in to Lieutenant Colonel Heinz Brandt, who was traveling with Hitler, and flashed a cool smile.

BRANDT, MIGHT I TROUBLE YOU TO DELIVER A PAIR OF BRANDY BOTTLES TO GENERAL STIEFF, WITH MY COMPLIMENTS?

The trusting Brandt accepted gladly. When the party reached the airfield, Schlabrendorff stealthily slipped his hand into the package and activated the acidic fuse. He nervously carried the bomb out to the plane, where the Führer waited to take off. He made a delicate hand-off with Lieutenant Colonel Brandt on the runway, After a pause, Brandt saluted and placed the bomb in the cargo compartment ... and Hitler's plane took OFF!

AFTER THEY GOT NEWS
THE PLOT WAS UNDERWAY ...

DIETRICH AND SOME OF THE OTHER CONSPIRATORS HUDDLED BY THE RADIO,

hoping to hear the first news bulletin that the Führer was dead. They waited and waited. Then, finally, a news report: Hitler had landed safely back at his command headquarters in East Prussia! THE PLOT HAD FAILED.

Dietrich and his friends were despondent. They worried they might never get such a chance again. And with each passing day, the Gestapo was closing in on them. But instead of fleeing Germany, they bravely went back to work crafting a new plot. The only way out of this trap was through the grave of Hitler's Reich.

THE STORY OF WHAT HAPPENED TO THAT BOMB IS MORE HARROWING THAN THE PLOT ITSELF. WHEN THE CONSPIRATORS REALIZED HITLER HAD SURVIVED, THEY FEARED THE BOMB HAD BEEN DISCOVERED. EVEN IF IT HADN'T, THE BOMB WAS PUTTING EVERYONE IN THE ORGANIZATION IN DANGER. PROOF OF THE CONSPIRACY WAS JUST SITTING WAITING TO BE FOUND. SOMEONE HAD TO FIND OUT WHERE THE BOMB WAS ... AND GO GET IT!

GENERAL TRESCKOW AFFECTED A CALM VOICE AND CALLED HITLER'S STAFF TO INQUIRE IF THE PACKAGE HAD INDEED BEEN DELIVERED. SOMEHOW, IT WAS STILL THERE! UNDER THE GUISE OF OFFICIAL BUSINESS HE IMMEDIATELY TOOK A PLANE TO EAST PRUSSIA. BUT, WAS THIS JUST A TRAP TO DRAW OUT THOSE PLOTTING AGAINST HITLER? THE NEXT DAY, SCHLABRENDORFF MUSTERED ALL

HIS COURAGE AND WENT TO PICK UP THE PACKAGE, ON THE PRETENSE HE HAD MISTAKENLY SENT THE WRONG ONE TO GENERAL STIEFF. THE EXCHANGE OF A NEW PACKAGE WITH BRANDY FOR THE ONE WITH THE BOMB WAS CASUAL AND FAST. IT SEEMED NO ONE FROM HITLER'S STAFF KNEW THE TRUE NATURE OF WHAT SCHLABRENDORFF WAS NOW CARRYING.

AFTER EXAMINING THE FAULTY BOMB THEY FOUND EVERYTHING WORKED, BUT NOT THE ACTUAL DETONATOR. THE COLD TEMPERATURE AT HIGH ALTITUDES MAY HAVE CAUSED THE MISFIRE. BUT, THANKS TO THE DARING RESCUE OF THE DUD, THE CONSPIRACY WAS SAVED FROM THE BRINK OF DISASTER.

VON GERSDORF

HIMMLER

GÖRING

Feeling the clammy breath of the Gestapo on the backs of their necks, the conspirators planned to make a second attempt on Hitler's life just two weeks later. Through its government connections, the Abwehr discovered that Hitler (along with Hermann Göring and Heinrich Himmler, two of his most notorious goons) would be in Berlin on March 21, doing a tour of captured Russian weapons. It was almost too good to be true! Knocking out three legs of the Nazi hierarchy in one blow would certainly topple the beast, hopefully once and for all.

HITLER

This new plan was very different. It would be a suicide mission. The brave soul who volunteered for this assignment would help usher in the new German future, but he'd never live to see it.

General Rudolf-Christoph Freiherr von Gersdorff volunteered to carry this heavy load, quite literally. Two bombs would be fastened inside the pockets of his bulky overcoat.

THE PLAN: AS VON GERSDORFF GAVE THE TOUR, HE WOULD ACTIVATE THE FUSES ON THE BOMBS. THE PLOTTERS WOULD SET THE DEVICE TO EXPLODE AFTER 10 MINUTES. THE TOUR WOULD HAVE TO LAST JUST ONE SECOND LONGER. IT WOULD BE THE END OF THE THIRD REICH, AND IT WOULD COST THE GENERAL HIS LIFE.

The day of the second attempt was a Sunday. Hans and the Bonhoeffer family had gathered at his sister Ursula's home at 41 Marienburger Allee, to practice a song together for Karl Bonhoeffer's seventy-fifth birthday. As they sang, Hans and Dietrich did their best to act normal. Occasionally they would catch each other's eye, as they kept an ear out for the phone to ring. Hans had parked his car right outside the front door, ready to leave at a moment's notice to begin building the new government. Once again, they waited and waited and waited.

Just a few miles away, Hitler had finished his speech and was led into the next part of the event, the tour. General Gersdorff made a grand display of welcome and shook the Führer's hand. With the other hand, he activated the fuse. Ten minutes, counting down. He just had to stay as close as possible to Hitler.

As the brave general prattled on about the newly developed Soviet tanks, particularly the T-34 ... the time was ticking away. The Nazi reign of evil, along with the general's own life, was coming to an end.

HE BRACED HIMSELF FOR THE BLAST.

Suddenly, without warning, Hitler left the tour early and quickly exited out a side door with his entourage! The planned half-hour tour had lasted only eight minutes. Gersdorff was stunned. Also, he was still wearing a coat with two active bombs in it! There was no way to turn off the timer! He quickly excused himself to the bathroom, and as fast as he could, he carefully ripped out the lining to the coat and pulled the fuses from the explosives just in time.

HE WAS ALIVE, BUT THE PLOT HAD FAILED.

HITLER HAD ESCAPED THE TRAP ONCE AGAIN!

DIETRICH AND HANS NEVER GOT
THE CALL THEY WERE WAITING FOR.

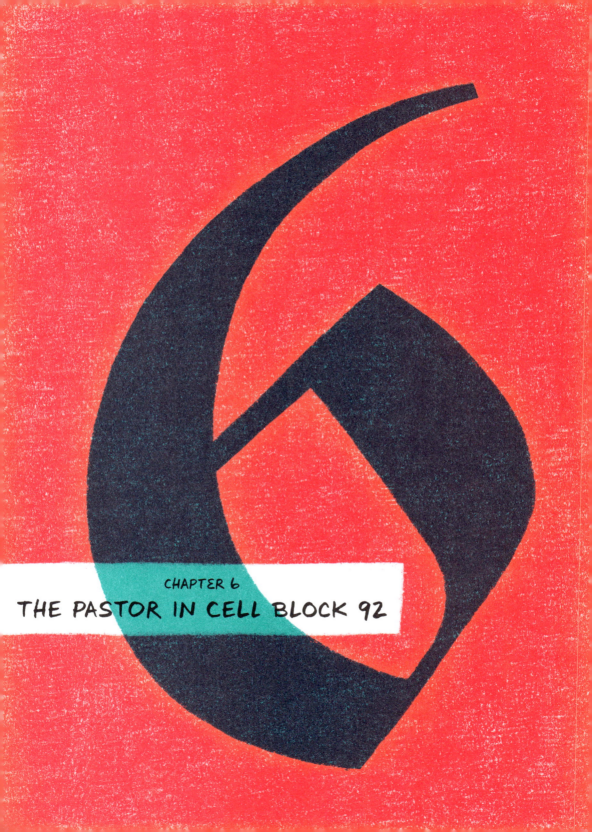

CHAPTER 6
THE PASTOR IN CELL BLOCK 92

IN 100 YEARS—IT WILL ALL BE OVER.

DIETRICH WAS ALONE.

Arrested two weeks after the failed plot against Hitler, he was now a prisoner of the Nazis. After two days in total isolation at Tegel Prison in western Berlin, the guards gave Dietrich his Bible. He was not allowed to see anyone. Dietrich wasn't even told why he had been arrested. It was dreadfully cold in the cell, and his blankets smelled of vomit and filth. At night, surrounded by the cries of his fellow prisoners, any semblance of sleep was near impossible.

On April 5, 1943, the Gestapo had come to the Bonhoeffer home with a warrant for his arrest. They had also arrested Hans and his wife, Christine, Dietrich's sister. Their arrests were part of a big plan by the Gestapo. For years, the Gestapo had jealously longed to expose its rival, the Abwehr, as a nest of treachery and corruption. Even though Hans and Dietrich had been arrested, the spies knew the game wasn't up. Charges were not brought, so it was possible the Gestapo might not have any hard evidence against them. The Gestapo often relied on frightening people to get what they wanted. Dietrich had guessed earlier that the plan was to separate him from Hans and make them suffer in hopes of getting them to confess to their crimes. Hans wasn't even at Tegel Prison but in a military detention center elsewhere in Berlin. Fortunately, Dietrich and Hans had anticipated this possibility and made careful plans to thwart the Gestapo's nasty strategy.

Both men had created elaborate stories together to explain their suspicious activity in the Abwehr. Working inside a spy agency gave them ample opportunities to explain that what they were doing was designed to look suspicious on purpose.

Dietrich had even created a fake diary that he placed in his room for the Gestapo to find upon his arrest. It gave a cover story for all his movements on behalf of the conspiracy. In fact, the Gestapo believed Operation 7 was a money-laundering scheme, not a covert Jew-smuggling plot. The Gestapo had no idea they had captured two parts of an assassination conspiracy against the Führer! At this point, the Gestapo's main targets were much higher up the chain of command at the Abwehr: General Oster and Admiral Canaris. Led by the Gestapo's senior military prosecutor, Manfred Roeder, they hoped to break Dietrich wide open, spilling out all the dirt on his commanding officers. What the Gestapo had expected to find was rampant embezzlement and misappropriation of resources. Little did they know how much more there was to this quiet pastor and his allies.

Dietrich spent twelve miserable days in solitary confinement, designed to break his spirit of resistance. It did no such thing. Before Hans and Dietrich were arrested, they created a strategy for this very moment:

"BE STRONG. ADMIT NOTHING."*

After a few grueling sessions of questioning with Roeder, Dietrich sensed the Gestapo was grasping at straws. Perhaps it was true: the Gestapo needed them to confirm their suspicions. Dietrich's role in the strategy was to never deny his basic beliefs but to play the part of a loyal German who had come to serve the Reich as best he could. He began to be hopeful that after a few weeks of this, he might be released.

Dietrich's time at Tegel was not as hard as his first twelve days might have indicated. The prison staff discovered that Dietrich was related to General Paul von Hase (his mother's cousin), the military commandant of Berlin. This changed his circumstances immediately! The solitary confinement ended, and the guards suddenly treated him like a celebrity. They also offered him larger portions of food, but Dietrich always refused in protest, rebuking the guards for not treating all the prisoners with equal care.

Dietrich was moved to cell block 92 in Tegel Prison. The change was quite dramatic. The cell offered a medium-sized window, better food, and most important, pen and paper. Dietrich was allowed to write letters now. Despite his terrible physical circumstances, the worst part had been the isolation from his love of communication. Now his family could send him packages and even come to visit occasionally. His parents would send him one parcel a week, including books, writing supplies, and fresh clothes.

Dietrich's cell slowly began to resemble the approximation of a home. On the wall, there was a reproduction of Dürer's "Apocalypse"—on his desk, books and candles. His window looked out over the prison yard, into a grove of pine trees.

On Sunday mornings, he could hear the distant church bells. If he hadn't known any better, the spartan quarters could have been his room at Finkenwalde.

"THE WIND SOMETIMES BEARS FRAGMENTS OF HYMNS TO ME."*

WHILE HE WAS AT TEGEL, DIETRICH NEVER ASSUMED THE POSTURE OF A TIMID PRISONER, OFTEN BERATING GUARDS FOR THEIR TERRIBLE BEHAVIOR TOWARD OTHERS. "IT MAKES ME FURIOUS TO SEE QUITE DEFENCELESS [SIC] PEOPLE BEING UNJUSTLY SHOUTED AT AND INSULTED. THESE PETTY TORMENTORS, WHO CAN RAGE LIKE THAT AND WHOM ONE FINDS EVERYWHERE, GET ME WORKED UP FOR HOURS ON END."*

Despite being suddenly jailed by the Nazis, Dietrich had not been cut off from the core network of the conspiracy. Thanks to careful planning, Dietrich and Hans had secretly created a way to send messages through the Bonhoeffer family, even after they were captured!

They had created a secret book code: Every time Dietrich was sent a new book, he knew to look for his name on the inside cover. If his name was underlined, the book carried a secret message. Next, he had to look for something on every third or every tenth page, starting from the back. Dietrich would search for the smallest pencil mark underneath a single letter, straining his eyes in the dim candlelight to find it. Then he would skip three or ten more pages and find another mark. Eventually, he could piece together a short message from Hans or the other spies at the Abwehr. Some of the messages that Dietrich received were like this one:

I-M N-O-T C-E-R-T-A-I-N T-H-A-T T-H-E L-E-T-T-E-R W-I-T-H H-A-N-S-S C-O-R-R-E-C-T-I-O-N H-A-S B-E-E-N F-O-U-N-D B-U-T T-H-I-N-K S-O.*

THESE NOTES WOULD HELP THE TWO MAKE SURE THEIR STORIES FOR THE INVESTIGATORS MATCHED PERFECTLY. IF THEY BOTH DENIED THEIR INVOLVEMENT IN THE SAME MANNER, IT WOULD HELP TO CONFIRM THEIR INNOCENCE.

DESPITE THE BETTER TREATMENT, DIETRICH STILL FELT ISOLATED FROM MARIA AND EBERHARD. HE WAS GIVEN PERMISSION TO WRITE ONE LETTER EVERY TEN DAYS, BUT ONLY TO MEMBERS OF HIS IMMEDIATE FAMILY. THESE LETTERS HAD TO PASS THROUGH THE CENSORS, WHO WOULD READ THE LETTERS TO LOOK FOR SUBVERSIVE OR SECRET INFORMATION. ANYTHING DEEMED SUSPICIOUS OR INAPPROPRIATE WOULD NOT BE SENT HOME, BUT FORWARDED ON TO THE GESTAPO. THE PROSECUTORS WERE EAGER TO USE ANY INFORMATION HE DIVULGED TO HIS FAMILY AGAINST HIM. DIETRICH HAD TO BE CAREFUL. HE COULDN'T EXPRESS HIS TRUE FEELINGS TO ANYONE. HE WORRIED

THAT MARIA WAS WORRIED ABOUT HIM. MARIA DID NOT YET LIVE IN BERLIN BUT SHE OCCASIONALLY CAME TO STAY WITH HIS PARENTS TO BE NEAR DIETRICH. DIETRICH BRAVELY TRIED TO REASSURE THEM THAT HE WAS SAFE AND CONFIDENT OF HIS RELEASE. BUT DEEP DOWN, HE WAS TROUBLED AND NEEDED A REAL FRIEND.

BEYOND THE FEAR AND UNCERTAINTY, THERE WAS AN INTENSE BOREDOM DIETRICH HAD NEVER EXPERIENCED BEFORE. HE WROTE TO HIS PARENTS THAT HE WAS PACING UP AND DOWN HIS CELL, CAGED "LIKE A POLAR BEAR."*

ALONG WITH THE BOOK CODE, DIETRICH'S FAMILY ALSO DISCOVERED THAT GLASS JAM JARS CONTAINED DOUBLE CARDBOARD LIDS UNDERNEATH THE CAPS—PERFECT FOR SENDING A TREAT TO DIETRICH AND FOR SMUGGLING SECRET MESSAGES! BY REMOVING THE FRONT PIECE, HIS MOTHER COULD HIDE A TINY MESSAGE BETWEEN THE TWO CARDBOARD BACKINGS.

A blessing came to Dietrich in the person of a sympathetic guard named Corporal Knobloch. Sadly, his first name has been lost to time. At a place like Tegel, both guards and prisoners were the forgotten castoffs of the Nazi machine. Even a guard might secretly harbor anti-Nazi sentiments. Knobloch, for his part, was also a man of faith and may have heard Dietrich preach before they met in prison. As Knobloch got to know the imprisoned pastor, he decided to help him. The corporal bravely volunteered to take any number of letters Dietrich wrote, stash them in his bag, and mail them from his house in Berlin, outside the prison walls. This way Dietrich could avoid the eyes of the censors. The conspiracy never used this risky channel to send covert information. But finally, after months of guarded communication, he could talk openly with Maria and his best friend from Finkenwalde, Eberhard.

Dietrich quickly became quite a curiosity at Tegel Prison. The guards all felt his presence there to be a bit bizarre. He just didn't fit the mold of the other prisoners; he was measured and kind. He seemed to be buoyed by a kind of inner strength that the others, even the guards, longed to possess. Dietrich became a kind of unofficial pastor to the entire prison. He would spend time counseling inmates in his cell, bringing comfort to those on the edge of despair. Ever since childhood, Dietrich had shown the heart of a shepherd. Now he was caring for the wayward sheep in his midst.

The rules began to bend around Dietrich quite a bit. The guards began to trust him enough to appoint him as an orderly in the prison infirmary. He enjoyed going to the sick bay, as it was a place where he really could be of service. Plus the guards would secretly listen to the BBC (British Broadcasting Corporation, originating from England) on the radio. The BBC gave a very different account of the war from what the German government was telling its people. Against all odds, Dietrich had become a dependable part of the prison's nerve structure, especially in moments of crisis.

After three months at Tegel, Dietrich began to realize it would be a long season of imprisonment. But he made the most of his time there, writing hundreds of letters, many poems, works of fiction, and theological explorations. His observations about the severity of prison life were some of the most poignant. He longed for simple things, like hearing laughter again.

JOY IS A THING THAT WE WANT VERY BADLY IN THIS SOLEMN BUILDING, WHERE ONE NEVER HEARS A LAUGH.*

MACHINE-WORKS FACTORY

THE WAR TOOK ITS FIRST MAJOR TURN AGAINST GERMANY IN THE SUMMER OF 1943. BERLIN HAD FALLEN UNDER THE ROUTINE OF DAY-AND-NIGHT ALLIED BOMBINGS. TEGEL PRISON WAS LOCATED DANGEROUSLY CLOSE TO A MACHINE-WORKS FACTORY, A DELICIOUS TARGET FOR BOMBING RAIDS. SUCH LITTLE THOUGHT WAS GIVEN TO THE PROTECTION OF NAZI PRISONERS (AND THEIR GUARDS) THAT TEGEL DIDN'T HAVE A SINGLE BOMB SHELTER.

TEGEL PRISON

Night after night, the air-raid siren would blare, sending the prisoners into fits of hysteria. Dietrich felt the same dread as his cell was lit up in the ghostly green light from the "christmas tree" flares the bombers used to illuminate their targets. Assisting the guards, he would quickly rush the prisoners to the most interior rooms of the prison. Moving throughout the din, he would pray with grown men awash in tears, as the blasts echoed around them for hours.

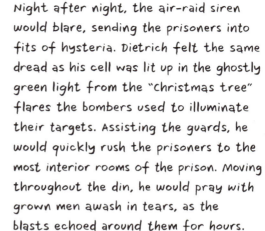

On one occasion a bomb fell so close that the windows of the infirmary were shattered around the cowering inmates. With the room exploding around him, Dietrich lay quietly on the floor praying, waiting for his death—holding the hands of his fellow prisoners.

LIFE IN CELL BLOCK 92 HAD TAKEN ON A MONASTIC QUALITY. DIETRICH WOULD WAKE EACH MORNING TO PRAYER, WITH A PSALM ON HIS LIPS FROM THE AIR RAID THE NIGHT BEFORE. THE GUARDS WOULD WANDER INTO HIS CELL IN THE DUSTY MORNING LIGHT FOR COMFORT.

PRAY FOR US, PASTOR, THAT WE MAY HAVE NO ALERTS TONIGHT.

EVERY FEW DAYS, DIETRICH WAS TAKEN INTO A DARK ROOM FOR ANOTHER ROUND OF QUESTIONING WITH ROEDER. HE CONTINUED TO HOLD FIRM AND PLAY HIS PART, PARRYING THE GESTAPO'S QUESTIONS AS BEST HE COULD. HIS MOTHER WOULD SEND FLOWERS FROM THEIR GARDEN TO BRIGHTEN HIS CELL, BUT THE SPECTER OF DEATH WAS EVERYWHERE.

WHILE WALKING IN THE PRISON YARD,

DIETRICH DISCOVERED A NEST OF BABY TOMTIT BIRDS. HE ENJOYED SEEING THEM ON HIS WALK EACH AFTERNOON.

ONE DAY HE DISCOVERED THE NEST DESTROYED AND SEVERAL DEAD BIRDS ON THE GROUND.

SOME CRUEL FELLOW WENT AND DESTROYED THE LOT. ... I CAN'T UNDERSTAND IT.*

HE SHOWED A STRONG FACE TO THOSE HE SERVED AT TEGEL, FERVENTLY PRAYING FOR THE AFFLICTED AROUND HIM: FOR HIS FELLOW PRISONERS, FOR THE GUARDS, AND FOR HIS ENEMIES. HIS CELL BECAME A KIND OF CONFESSIONAL. IT WAS A RESPITE OF PEACE FOR THOSE WHO WERE LOST IN THE NAZI CHAOS.

BUT HIS FAITH FELT SMALL. EVEN EMPTY.

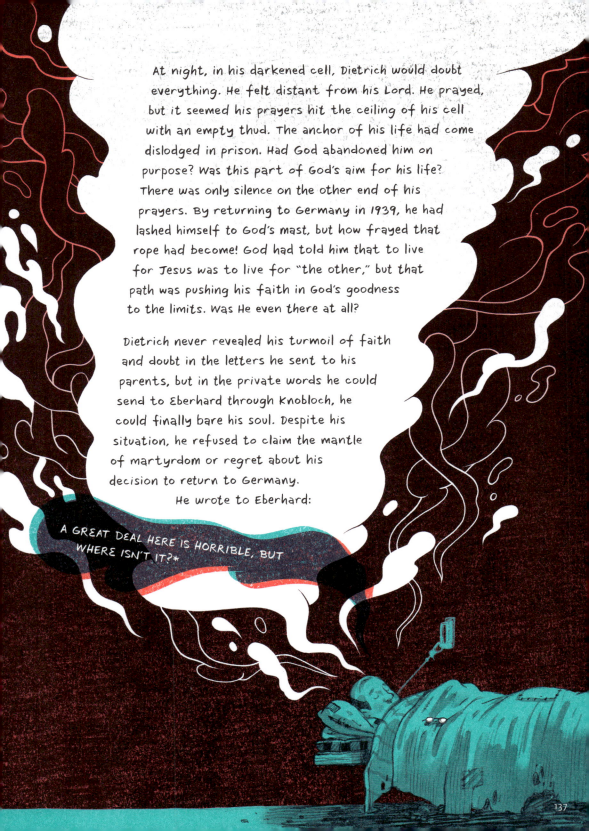

At night, in his darkened cell, Dietrich would doubt
everything. He felt distant from his Lord. He prayed,
but it seemed his prayers hit the ceiling of his cell
with an empty thud. The anchor of his life had come
dislodged in prison. Had God abandoned him on
purpose? Was this part of God's aim for his life?
There was only silence on the other end of his
prayers. By returning to Germany in 1939, he had
lashed himself to God's mast, but how frayed that
rope had become! God had told him that to live
for Jesus was to live for "the other," but that
path was pushing his faith in God's goodness
to the limits. Was He even there at all?

Dietrich never revealed his turmoil of faith
and doubt in the letters he sent to his
parents, but in the private words he could
send to Eberhard through Knobloch, he
could finally bare his soul. Despite his
situation, he refused to claim the mantle
of martyrdom or regret about his
decision to return to Germany.
  He wrote to Eberhard:

A GREAT DEAL HERE IS HORRIBLE, BUT
WHERE ISN'T IT?*

Dietrich continued to hope his freedom would come any day, but the ominous weight of his circumstance was inescapable.

MY GRIM EXPERIENCES OFTEN PURSUE ME INTO THE NIGHT AND ... I CAN SHAKE THEM OFF ONLY BY RECITING ONE HYMN AFTER ANOTHER, AND ... I'M APT TO WAKE WITH A SIGH RATHER THAN A HYMN OF PRAISE*

AND THEN THERE WAS MARIA.

His quiet routine of prison life was occasionally broken by a surprising interlude of grace. Dietrich would be led from his cell by a guard, made to believe he was going to face another Gestapo interrogation, when the door would open and there was beautiful Maria. They could speak for only a few short minutes, never touching each other, always under the supervision of a Nazi minder. (Even these visits by Maria were designed by the Gestapo to crush his spirit.) But merely the sight of her face and the sound of her voice were enough to remind him he had a future beyond the Nazis. Those sudden minutes would sustain a hope in Dietrich for weeks to come. Her visits were also bittersweet, a reminder of how much he was losing in cell 92.

"In my experience, nothing tortures us more than longing,"* he wrote to Eberhard.

Months after his arrest, in July 1943, Dietrich was finally told the charges against him: "Evasion of military duty and assisting others to do the same." Even though this charge was very serious, given what it could have been, it was a huge relief. At this time, Dietrich was now convinced that Hans had covered their tracks so well that release would be inevitable. But the problem with any kind of assumption about the Nazi hierarchy was underestimating their rampant paranoia. Their suspicions were arbitrary and unpredictable. Yet he had a real reason to hope once again.

The routine Gestapo interrogations became more and more vicious, as his captors grew desperate to find a weak spot in Dietrich's defenses. The questioning from Roeder was related only to his past as a thorn in the side of the Reich church, and not directly about his covert work in the Abwehr. Astonishingly, nothing definitive had been discovered about his role in Operation 7! It seemed Dietrich had done the impossible and darted through the advancing Nazi Blitzkrieg. Might he actually escape?

JUST A FEW MILES AWAY, IN THE REICH CHANCELLERY HEADQUARTERS, HITLER WAS LEARNING THAT HIS WAR WAS NOT GOING WELL. HIS GAMBLE IN OPENING ANOTHER WAR ON THE EASTERN FRONT HAD FINALLY COLLAPSED. AT THIS POINT, IN LATE 1943, THE GERMAN FORCES WERE IN A COMPLETELY DEFENSIVE POSTURE. NEVER AGAIN IN THE WAR WOULD GERMANY BE ON THE OFFENSIVE OR GAIN NEW TERRITORY. THE WAR FELL INTO A FAMILIAR ROUTINE: FIGHT VICIOUSLY FOR WEEKS TO HOLD THE FRONT LINES, ONLY TO RETREAT, DIG IN THEIR HEELS, AND REPEAT.

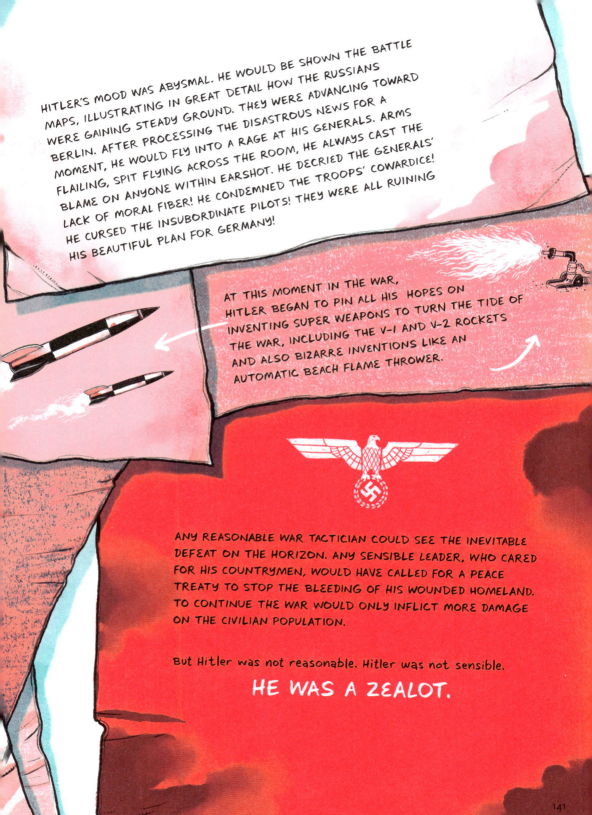

HITLER'S MOOD WAS ABYSMAL. HE WOULD BE SHOWN THE BATTLE MAPS, ILLUSTRATING IN GREAT DETAIL HOW THE RUSSIANS WERE GAINING STEADY GROUND. THEY WERE ADVANCING TOWARD BERLIN. AFTER PROCESSING THE DISASTROUS NEWS FOR A MOMENT, HE WOULD FLY INTO A RAGE AT HIS GENERALS. ARMS FLAILING, SPIT FLYING ACROSS THE ROOM, HE ALWAYS CAST THE BLAME ON ANYONE WITHIN EARSHOT. HE DECRIED THE GENERALS' LACK OF MORAL FIBER! HE CONDEMNED THE TROOPS' COWARDICE! HE CURSED THE INSUBORDINATE PILOTS! THEY WERE ALL RUINING HIS BEAUTIFUL PLAN FOR GERMANY!

AT THIS MOMENT IN THE WAR, HITLER BEGAN TO PIN ALL HIS HOPES ON INVENTING SUPER WEAPONS TO TURN THE TIDE OF THE WAR, INCLUDING THE V-1 AND V-2 ROCKETS AND ALSO BIZARRE INVENTIONS LIKE AN AUTOMATIC BEACH FLAME THROWER.

ANY REASONABLE WAR TACTICIAN COULD SEE THE INEVITABLE DEFEAT ON THE HORIZON. ANY SENSIBLE LEADER, WHO CARED FOR HIS COUNTRYMEN, WOULD HAVE CALLED FOR A PEACE TREATY TO STOP THE BLEEDING OF HIS WOUNDED HOMELAND. TO CONTINUE THE WAR WOULD ONLY INFLICT MORE DAMAGE ON THE CIVILIAN POPULATION.

But Hitler was not reasonable. Hitler was not sensible.

HE WAS A ZEALOT.

WE FIGHT TO THE LAST MAN!
IF GERMANY CANNOT WIN, THEN **EVERYTHING SHOULD PERISH WITH US!**

HITLER THUNDERED AWAY.

HITLER COMMANDED HIS MEN TO FIGHT THE LOSING BATTLE UNTIL THERE WAS NOTHING LEFT OF GERMANY. HE DUMPED THEM INTO THE MEAT GRINDER, LEAVING NOTHING BUT A BLOODY PULP. HE EVEN TOLD HIS TROOPS THAT IN RETREATING, THEY MUST DESTROY GERMAN TOWNS, BRIDGES, AND FACTORIES, SO THE ENEMY COULD CLAIM NOTHING BUT A BURNED HUSK.

THE GENERALS REALIZED IT WAS TOO LATE TO VINDICATE GERMANY, EVEN WITH A SUCCESSFUL ASSASSINATION. BUT ...IT MIGHT NOT BE TOO LATE TO SAVE THE PEOPLE OF GERMANY FROM COMPLETE ANNIHILATION. BY NOW, THE MASS EXTERMINATIONS OF THE HOLOCAUST WERE IN RELENTLESS OPERATION. HITLER WAS FAITHFULLY CARRYING OUT HEYDRICH'S PLAN, "THE FINAL SOLUTION," TO GET RID OF WHAT THEY CALLED "THE HUMAN FILTH." HISTORIANS ESTIMATE BY THE END OF THE WAR ROUGHLY 6 MILLION JEWS, AND 5 MILLION PEOPLE OF OTHER ETHNIC MINORITIES AND PRISONERS, WERE EXECUTED BY THE NAZIS. THOUGH THE CONSPIRATORS DIDN'T KNOW THE FULL EXTENT, EACH DAY THAT WENT BY MEANT THE LOSS OF TENS OF THOUSANDS OF LIVES—SOLDIERS, CIVILIANS, AND VICTIMS OF THE GENOCIDE.

THE REBELS HAD TIME, PERHAPS, FOR ONE LAST CHANCE TO ACT.

A FINAL PLAN TO ASSASSINATE HITLER WAS PUT INTO MOTION,

OPERATION VALKYRIE.

A suitcase bomb would be planted in one of Hitler's planning bunkers. The small confined concrete space would magnify the blast, killing everyone inside instantly. They wouldn't need a big bomb, just one in the right place. Of all the plots that came before, this was the most complicated, and it was also the most dangerous.

In February 1944, Maria showed up at Tegel on Dietrich's thirty-eighth birthday.

Maria's visit was a delight, but she brought Dietrich a book that contained some coded bad news: Admiral Canaris, his ally in the conspiracy and the top man at the Abwehr, had been dismissed from his position. This could mean disaster for Dietrich—perhaps the Gestapo had found something Hans had forgotten about? Dietrich also learned that Hans's questioning at the detention center was indeed quickly progressing toward an actual trial date. These were both very bad omens for the captured spies.

With canaris removed, a young colonel named Claus von Stauffenberg stepped into leadership of the Abwehr Circle. Through the secret codes, Dietrich learned that Stauffenberg would lead the Valkyrie plot, but when would it happen? Hans and Dietrich just had to make it until Valkyrie could be carried out. With Hans's prosecution on the horizon,

CLAUS VON STAUFFENBERG

they needed an immediate way to delay the trial. In a brave stroke of genius to protect himself and Dietrich, Hans volunteered to infect himself with scarlet fever and diphtheria. Dietrich's sister Christine had managed to smuggle an infected swab to Hans with a secret note that read

RED PAPER AND STAIN ON THE MUG ...
=INFECTED!*

Hans was so sickened, he lost the ability to move his arms and legs and had to be transferred out of the prison to a military quarantine. The plan worked. His trial was postponed till he recovered. Now they needed the men of Operation Valkyrie to strike.

IT'S TIME NOW FOR SOMETHING TO BE DONE. HE WHO HAS THE COURAGE TO ACT MUST KNOW THAT HE WILL PROBABLY GO DOWN IN GERMAN HISTORY AS A TRAITOR. BUT, IF HE FAILS TO ACT, HE WILL BE A TRAITOR BEFORE HIS OWN CONSCIENCE.*   —CLAUS VON STAUFFENBERG

Von Stauffenberg was summoned by Hitler to meet with him in his secret Prussian headquarters, called the Wolfsschanze, or the Wolf's Lair. He boarded a plane in Berlin with his assistant, Lieutenant Werner von Haeften. Dietrich had personally counseled Werner about the morality of assassination a year earlier.

Claus carried a briefcase. Inside it were two bombs tightly packed inside a shirt and the papers for Stauffenberg's presentation to the Führer. Once the plane landed, Claus was formally escorted into the outpost.

THE WOLF'S LAIR WASN'T JUST A BUNKER BUT AN INTIMIDATING FORTIFICATION. TO GET INSIDE YOU HAD TO GET PAST:

AND FINALLY, A DETACHMENT OF ARMED SS GUARDS.

ELECTRIC BARB-WIRED FENCES,

PILLBOX MACHINE GUNS,

A MASSIVE MINEFIELD,

145

WOLF'S LAIR AIRPORT

Getting in wasn't a problem for von Stauffenberg. It was getting out that would be the challenge. Claus was an essential part of the group that planned to lead Germany after Hitler. Once the bomb detonated, he had to escape. His only chance was to use the immediate pandemonium following the blast to slip out undetected. The entire plan seemed to rely exclusively on good luck.

Valkyrie wasn't just a bombing. The operation was an entire military takeover. Once Hitler's inner circle had been crippled by Claus von Stauffenberg, the next step would go into action. The conspiracy had another man inside the Wolf's Lair, General Erich Fellgiebel, the chief of signals in the communications office. He would cut off all communication between the headquarters and Berlin. Once it was radioed to Berlin that the bomb had worked and Hitler was dead, Valkyrie could truly begin. The other generals in the conspiracy would use Berlin's reserve army to take over command in the capital. Then they would command these reserve officers to arrest all the SS members along with the Nazi elite, on the pretense of a "failed coup." In fact, the generals giving the commands were the actual coup!

When von Stauffenberg drove into the Wolf's Lair, the plan changed—before it even started. He was dismayed to hear the meeting would not be held in the underground bunker because of the extreme heat. It was moved to an open-windowed conference room. Now the explosive would have to be right next to Hitler. Stauffenberg could not rely on the dense bunker walls to magnify the damage.

WOLF'S LAIR

BERLIN

12:30 pm CLAUS AND GENERAL WILHELM KEITEL (THE HEAD OF THE WEHRMACHT) WERE RUNNING LATE FOR THE MEETING, BUT STAUFFENBERG MADE A SUDDEN EXCUSE TO ADJUST HIS UNIFORM, ANNOYING KEITEL. HE CAREFULLY REMOVED THE BOMBS AND STRUGGLED TO ACTIVATE BOTH DETONATORS.

12:32 pm CLAUS HAD LOST AN EYE, HIS RIGHT HAND, AND PART OF HIS LEFT HAND IN THE NAZI TANK BATTLES OF NORTH AFRICA, MAKING ACTIVATION DIFFICULT. THE PUNCTUAL GENERAL KEITEL WAS IMPATIENT.

COLONEL? LET'S GO! THE MEETING HAS STARTED!

FUMBLING WITH HIS REMAINING THREE FINGERS, CLAUS COULD ARM ONLY ONE OF THE TWO BOMBS.

ONE SHOULD BE ENOUGH.

12:35 pm CLAUS TOOK HIS PLACE AT THE TABLE, MAKING AN APOLOGETIC GESTURE TO HITLER FOR ENTERING THE MEETING LATE. HE CAREFULLY SET DOWN HIS BRIEFCASE BOMB BY THE TABLE. WHILE STANDING AT ATTENTION WITH THE OTHER OFFICERS, HE SLID THE BOMB UNDER THE TABLE WITH HIS FEET, NEARER TO THE FÜHRER.

12:36 pm
12:37 pm
12:38 pm

<<TICK-TICK-TICK>>

12:39 pm IT WAS TIME TO GO! THE FUSE WAS SHORT, SET TO ONLY 10 MINUTES. CLAUS QUIETLY EXCUSED HIMSELF TO MAKE AN URGENT CALL TO BERLIN TO "UPDATE THE INFORMATION FOR HIS REPORT."

12:42 pm IT WAS HIGHLY IRREGULAR TO LEAVE HITLER'S PRESENCE WITHOUT BEING DISMISSED, BUT IT WORKED. NO ONE SEEMED ALARMED. AS HE EXITED THE MEETING HALL, HE WALKED AS FAST AS HE COULD WITHOUT AROUSING SUSPICIONS WHEN—

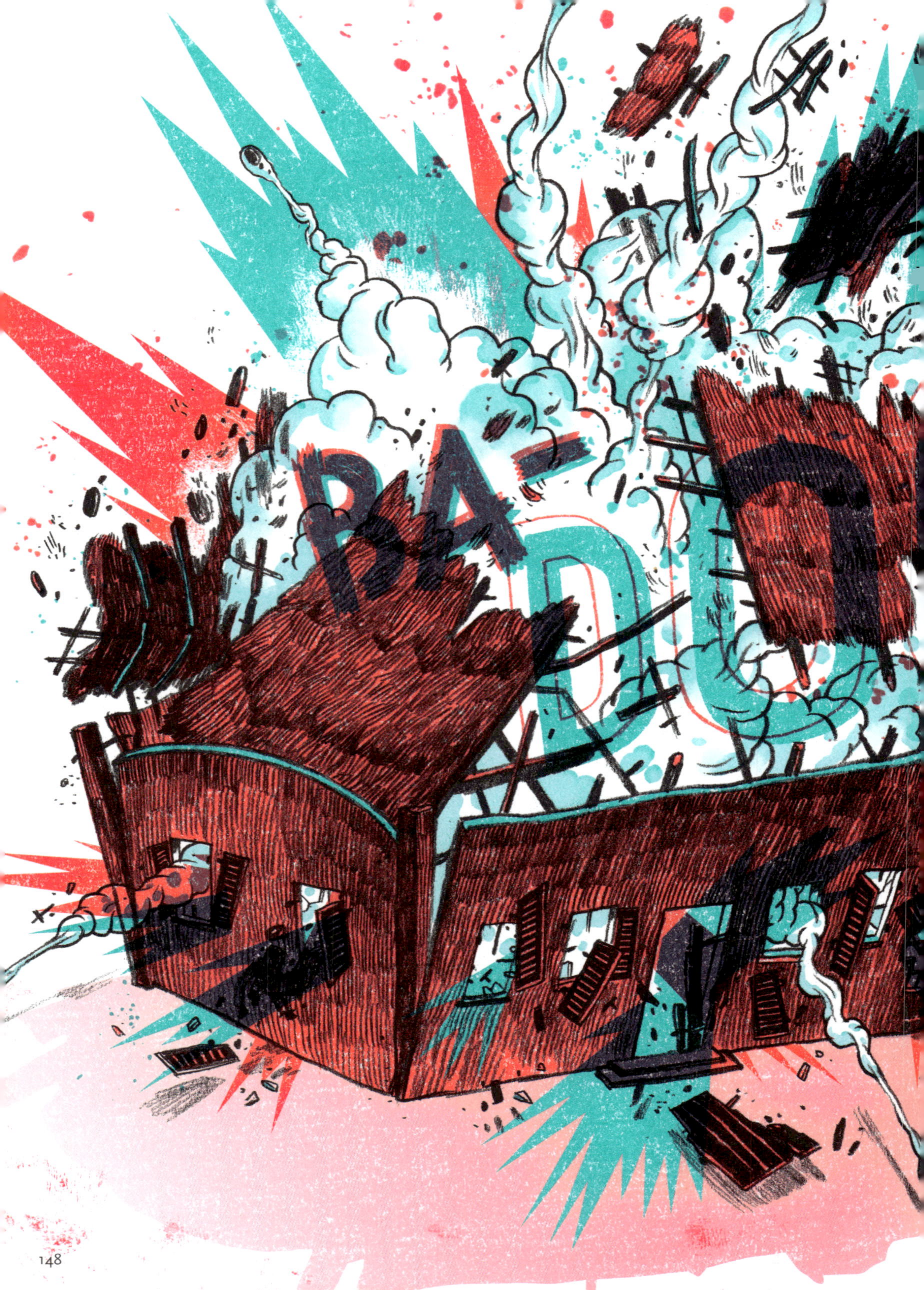
BA-

HE TURNED TO SEE FLAMES, DEBRIS, AND MEN FLYING OUT OF THE WINDOWS. EVERYWHERE AROUND HIM, IT WAS TOTAL HYSTERIA!

The ensuing chaos gave Claus enough cover to escape the fortress, just as he had hoped. General Erich Fellgiebel saw the blast and radioed Berlin, "The bomb has gone off—activate valkyrie." Then he disabled the phone and radio lines from the Wolf's Lair, giving the generals in Berlin time to do their part. Moments later, back at the airport, Claus took off in his plane for Berlin—for the capital of the new Germany. At the airport, von Stauffenberg said about Hitler:

"FATE HAS OFFERED US THIS OPPORTUNITY, AND I WOULD NOT REFUSE IT FOR ANYTHING IN THE WORLD. I HAVE SEARCHED MY CONSCIENCE, BEFORE GOD AND BEFORE MYSELF. THIS MAN IS EVIL INCARNATE."*

Everything in the plot had worked perfectly, except for one critical detail.

HITLER HAD SURVIVED.

THE PANTS ADOLF HITLER WAS WEARING AT THE TIME WERE SHREDDED BEYOND RECOGNITION BY THE BLAST. HE SAVED THESE PANTS AND HAD THEM SENT TO HIS MISTRESS, EVA BRAUN, AS PROOF OF GOD'S BLESSING ON HIS LEADERSHIP.

Valkyrie could not work unless
Hitler was dead. In a twist of fate,
he was barely injured. The suitcase
with the bomb, moments before it
exploded, had been moved away from Hitler behind a
giant wooden table divider by Colonel Heinz Brandt.
The divider was sturdy enough to deflect the blast
away from the Führer. The explosion killed four in
the meeting, but Hitler escaped with only singed hair,
tattered pants, and burst eardrums.

THIS CASUAL MOVE
BY COLONEL BRANDT
SAVED HITLER'S LIFE AND
COST THE MAN HIS OWN.
IRONICALLY, BRANDT
WAS THE OFFICER WHO
UNKNOWINGLY TRANSPORTED
THE BRANDY BOMB IN
OPERATION FLASH A
YEAR EARLIER.

Claus von Stauffenberg landed in Berlin three hours later and
immediately telephoned the command center to check on the progress
of the government takeover. It had not even started! General Fellgiebel's
initial word of the blast had been garbled over the radio, and the
Berlin conspirators delayed starting the takeover in confusion.

Then, disaster. Survivors from the Wolf's Lair contacted Berlin: Hitler
was alive and had given orders to arrest Claus von Stauffenberg.
Claus rallied his commanders and bravely went ahead with the coup.
By the evening, the SS and the army reserve men had realized the
trap and swarmed the conspirators. Werner von Haeften, Claus von
Stauffenberg, and the other ringleaders were captured and executed
by firing squad on the spot. His last words were:

"LONG LIVE OUR SACRED GERMANY!"*

THE PLOT HAD FAILED ... AGAIN.
THERE WOULD NOT BE ANOTHER.

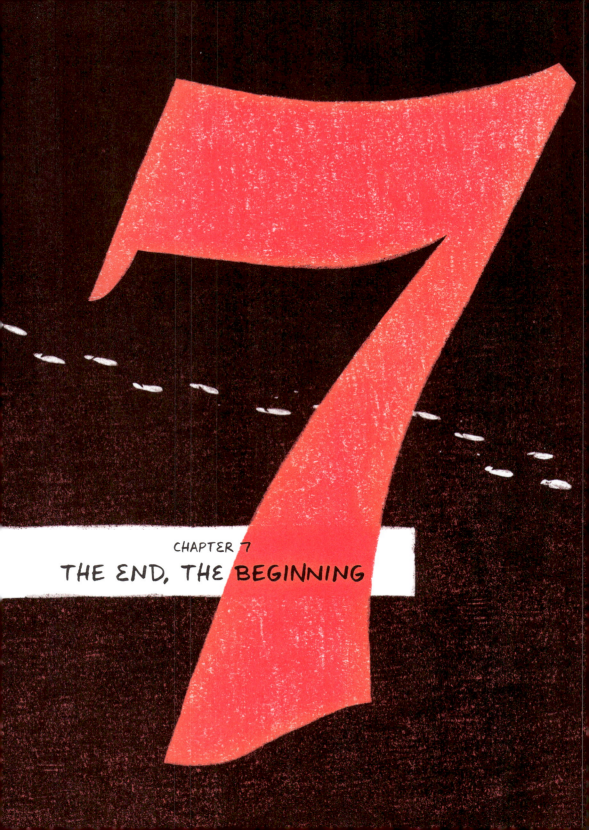

CHAPTER 7
THE END, THE BEGINNING

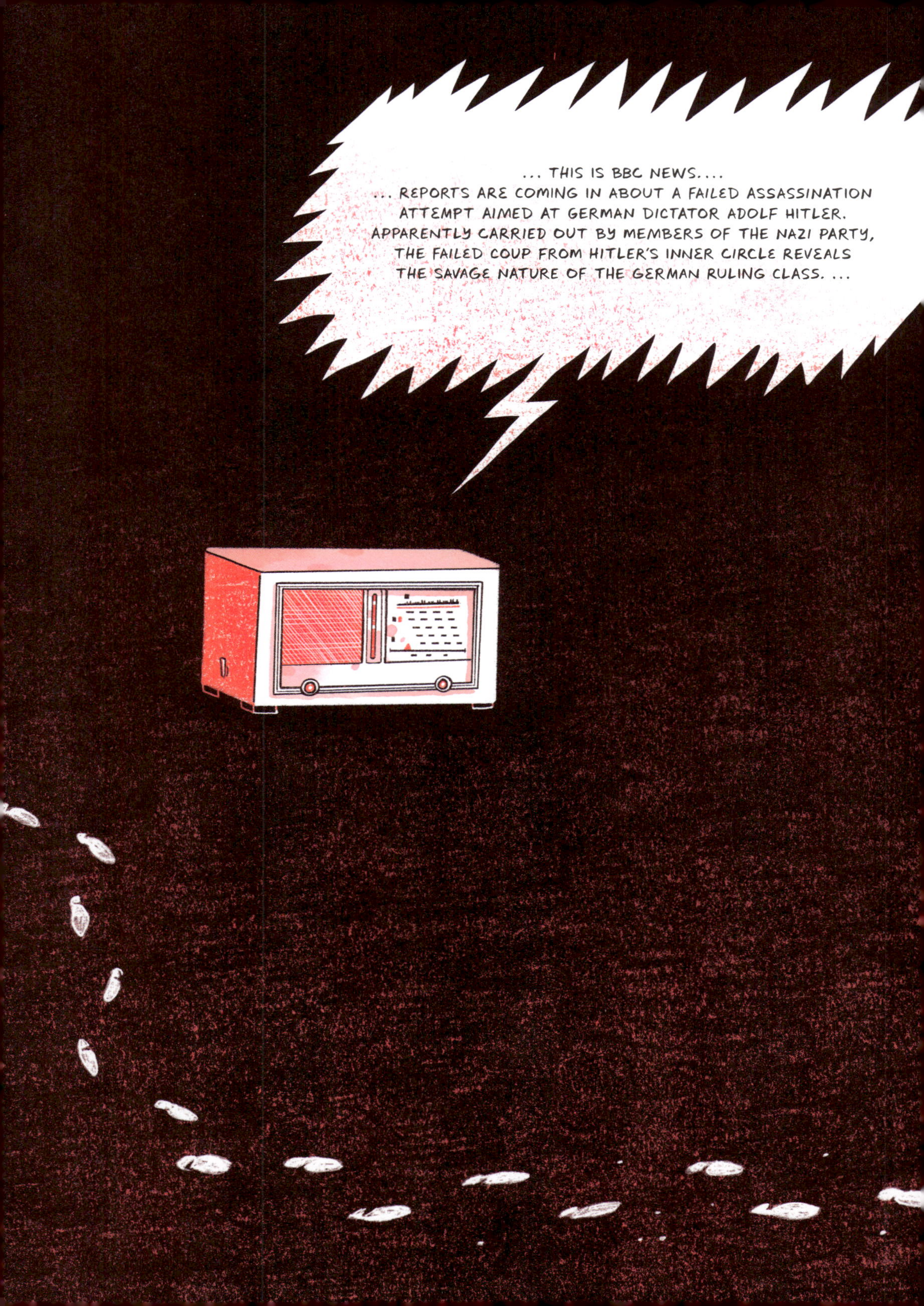
... THIS IS BBC NEWS....
... REPORTS ARE COMING IN ABOUT A FAILED ASSASSINATION ATTEMPT AIMED AT GERMAN DICTATOR ADOLF HITLER. APPARENTLY CARRIED OUT BY MEMBERS OF THE NAZI PARTY, THE FAILED COUP FROM HITLER'S INNER CIRCLE REVEALS THE SAVAGE NATURE OF THE GERMAN RULING CLASS. ...

EVERYTHING WAS COMING UNRAVELED.

JULY 23, 1944

Dietrich hears Admiral Canaris was arrested.

AUGUST 8, 1944

General Paul von Hase, Dietrich's "Uncle Paul," was hanged at Plötzensee Prison along with eight other Valkyrie conspirators.

AUGUST 22, 1944

Hans von Dohnányi, Dietrich's closest ally in the conspiracy, was taken to Sachsenhausen concentration camp.

AUGUST 23, 1944

Maria visited Dietrich. Without warning, Prosecutor Roeder stood her up and led her by the arm out of the room. She suddenly wrenched her arm away and rushed across the room, into Dietrich's arms.

During the first month after the failed Valkyrie plot, many thousands were arrested, some who had very little connection to the assassination. Hitler's white-hot rage was directed at the German elite for their heresy. For Hitler, to attack the Führer was to attack God himself! Hundreds were executed instantly. He left a few alive to be put through a very public shaming trial orchestrated by the Nazi chief judge, Roland Freisler, for propaganda purposes.

SEPTEMBER 20, 1944

Until this day, final confirmation of Dietrich's connection to the conspiracy had still been hidden. That all changed when the Gestapo found the Zossen files, the Abwehr's secret record of Nazi atrocities. Inside those files was a handwritten note from Dietrich. It directly linked him to the Abwehr traitors.

OCTOBER 1, 1944

Klaus Bonhoeffer, Dietrich's older brother, was arrested.

OCTOBER 4, 1944

Rüdiger Schleicher, Dietrich's brother-in-law, was arrested.

Life in Tegel Prison had evolved to allow Dietrich many unusual freedoms. One of those bizarre opportunities was the relative ease of a potential escape.

His friendship with Corporal Knobloch (who mailed his letters) had made the possibility of being smuggled out of Tegel a real option. Up until this point, the risks that came with a flight from Nazi capture were just too great, especially if the downfall of the Reich was imminent. With all that was happening in Berlin, he was probably safer in jail than on the run. The fallout from the failure of Valkyrie had changed the equation. If he wanted to escape, it would have to be now. Now or never.

Dietrich spoke with Knobloch and decided to make an escape. Knobloch would need to make the arrangements and to alert his family that he would be on the run. Even as Dietrich said the word "escape," he felt a familiar ache.

Who would have to pay for his flight from the Gestapo? Whom would he endanger? The list was long: his parents, Maria, his sisters, his nieces, his friends, his friends' wives and children. Dietrich wondered if his life was really worth more than those of his loved ones. Every day he was unaccounted for might mean a torture session for one of his most beloved. How could he, after all this, choose "self" over "other"? No. He could not run. He would stay. He would walk into the fire, eyes wide open.

Dietrich came to realize that what God had called him to was, ultimately, not success, but obedience.

"THE ULTIMATE QUESTION FOR A RESPONSIBLE MAN TO ASK IS NOT HOW HE IS TO EXTRICATE HIMSELF HEROICALLY FROM THE AFFAIR, BUT HOW THE COMING GENERATION IS GOING TO LIVE."*

OCTOBER 8, 1944

Dietrich was transferred from Tegel Prison to the SS prison at Gestapo Headquarters. He knew immediately it was very different from the place he had spent the last eighteen months. This SS prison was a notorious place of torture and isolation. His Bible was confiscated along with all his freedom of correspondence. He could write to his family, but not often, and no visitors were ever allowed. With him in this rat hole were the very worst enemies of the Nazi state. Even so, Dietrich was stunned to see Maria's cousin by marriage, fellow conspirator Fabian von Schlabrendorff in line with the other prisoners one morning. It was both so good and so tragic to see him in this place. It seemed the only thing here ahead of them both was misery.

DIETRICH BONHOEFFER HAD, THROUGH HIS LIFE'S WRITINGS AND NOW HIS DEEDS, REFRAMED THE CHRISTIAN LIFE THROUGH A LENS OF ACTION. HE CALLED FOR A RADICAL OBEDIENCE THAT WAS NOT CHEAP BUT COSTLY. FAITH WASN'T JUST ABOUT CREATING A SET OF COMFORTING THOUGHTS ABOUT GOD; IT WAS LIVING OUT AN ETHIC THAT CALLED FOR SACRIFICE. YOU DIDN'T JUST PRAY FOR THE TANKS TO STOP ROLLING,

YOU THREW YOURSELF IN FRONT OF THEM.

Dietrich never needed
that resolve more than at
this moment. The calculated
restraint from his new interrogators was
gone. The gloves came off, and the SS was free
to use any methods to get the answers to root out
the traitors. Maria's cousin Fabian, who survived the war,
described chilling sequences of physical torture and ridicule they
both had to endure. Of Dietrich, he said, "He was determined to
resist all the efforts of the Gestapo, and to reveal nothing. ... He
always cheered me up and comforted me, he never tired of repeating
that the only fight which is lost is that which we give up."*

Dietrich's conception of the nature of evil had changed. In the form of
the Nazi ideology, evil could no longer be a theological tool. The rigid
concepts of simple "right" and "wrong" had proved too simple for
defeating Hitler. Those stark boxes were all too easy for Hitler to
escape. Evil had totally surrounded Dietrich and the conspirators. On all
sides were ethical booby traps. Yet he had come to believe he must step
into one, if he was to act at all.

IF WE WANT TO BE CHRISTIANS,
WE MUST HAVE SOME SHARE
IN CHRIST'S LARGE-HEARTEDNESS
BY ACTING WITH RESPONSIBILITY
AND IN FREEDOM WHEN THE
MOMENT OF DANGER COMES. ...
MERE WAITING AND LOOKING ON
IS NOT CHRISTIAN BEHAVIOR.*

The action he had chosen was to stand fast in prison.
And now he must "suffer faithfully,"* as he called it.
He could see the end coming.

I DO NOT THINK THAT DEATH CAN TAKE US BY SURPRISE NOW.
AFTER WHAT WE HAVE BEEN THROUGH DURING THE WAR, WE HARDLY
DARE ADMIT THAT WE SHOULD LIKE DEATH TO COME TO US, NOT
ACCIDENTALLY AND SUDDENLY THROUGH SOME TRIVIAL CAUSE, BUT
IN THE FULNESS [SIC] OF LIFE AND WITH EVERYTHING AT STAKE.
IT IS WE OURSELVES, AND NOT OUTWARD CIRCUMSTANCES, WHO
MAKE DEATH WHAT IT CAN BE, A DEATH FREELY AND
VOLUNTARILY ACCEPTED.*

As Dietrich walked closer and closer toward
the end, something had changed besides his
circumstance. The Lord's presence fully
returned to him. His time at Tegel had
often felt like he was walking through
a dried-up ocean.

But
now the
parched earth
had been filled with a
heavenly rain. He filled his cup to
the brim and let it overflow in the
heavenly waters. In his final letter
to Maria, he wrote:

" ... WORDS FROM THE BIBLE, DISCUSSIONS LONG PAST, PIECES
OF MUSIC, AND BOOKS—ALL THESE GAIN LIFE AND REALITY AS
NEVER BEFORE. IT IS A GREAT INVISIBLE SPHERE IN WHICH ONE LIVES
AND IN WHOSE REALITY THERE IS NO DOUBT. IF IT SAYS IN THE OLD
CHILDREN'S SONG ABOUT THE ANGELS: 'TWO, TO COVER ME,
TWO TO WAKE ME,' SO IS THIS GUARDIANSHIP BY GOOD
INVISIBLE POWERS IN THE MORNING AND AT NIGHT."*
—DECEMBER 19, 1944

FEBRUARY 2, 1945 † †

Judge Roland Freisler of the People's Court sentenced Klaus Bonhoeffer and Rüdiger Schleicher to death.

FEBRUARY 7, 1945

A day after his thirty-ninth birthday, Dietrich was transferred from the SS prison in Berlin to Buchenwald concentration camp, 200 miles south of Berlin. A few days earlier, on February 3, an allied bomb had made a direct hit on the Berlin prison, forcing the transfer of all surviving prisoners. Dietrich was shackled and thrown into a transport van along with other colossal figures in the resistance, including Admiral Canaris and General Oster.

At Buchenwald, Dietrich lived a severe kind of existence, with little edible food and cold nights on a wooden plank bed. His chance for escape was gone; the only hope was to wait for the end, either his own or that of the Third Reich. He was held there for two months.

APRIL 1, 1945

Dietrich woke early, on Easter Sunday, to the sound of heavy guns beyond the horizon. The advancing Allied invasion had finally arrived. As the attack began to threaten Buchenwald, the guards were forced to evacuate the prisoners once again.

APRIL 3, 1945

DIETRICH AND FIFTEEN OTHER PRISONERS WERE HUDDLED INTO A TINY VAN POWERED BY A WOOD-BURNING GENERATOR. THEY ALL HAD TO SIT ON A MASSIVE PILE OF WOOD IN THE BACK, CHOKING ON EXHAUST FUMES, ON THEIR WAY TO THE NEXT DREADED DESTINATION: FLOSSENBÜRG CONCENTRATION CAMP. THIS RAGTAG GROUP OF PRISONERS AND GUARDS MADE A BIZARRE ROAD TRIP THROUGH SOUTHERN GERMANY. BUT WHEN THEY FINALLY MADE IT TO THE CONCENTRATION CAMP, THE GUARDS AT FLOSSENBÜRG REFUSED TO TAKE THE NEW PRISONERS! AFTER DAYS OF SEARCHING FOR A PLACE TO DUMP THEIR HUMAN CARGO, THE NAZI GUARDS FINALLY FOUND A SCHOOL BUILDING IN THE BAVARIAN VILLAGE OF SCHÖNBERG. DIETRICH BEGAN TO WONDER, WAS IT POSSIBLE THAT HE WOULD ESCAPE? DIETRICH WAS FAR AWAY FROM THE WAR, AND NOW FAR FROM THE EXECUTION CAMPS TOO. THE GUARDS WERE GROWING DESPONDENT. IT SEEMED THEIR CAPTORS MIGHT EVEN JUST RUN AWAY AND LEAVE THE PRISONERS TO FEND FOR THEMSELVES.

Holed up in an underground safe house called the Führerbunker, Adolf Hitler was handed the journals of Admiral Canaris. These books, part of the Zossen files that had been, until then, undiscovered, had been found in an abandoned safe the day before in the former Abwehr offices.

They revealed everything: direct treason, hatred for Hitler, and the Abwehr participation in multiple assassination attempts, including the Valkyrie plot. Heaving the journals across the room, he ordered the immediate execution of everyone arrested in connection with the Abwehr.

DESTROY THE CONSPIRATORS!

he yelled, as spittle flew onto those around him. Hitler had given the command for Dietrich Bonhoeffer's death.

Dietrich woke early, the Sunday after Easter, in the provincial schoolhouse alongside his fellow prisoners. They asked if he might hold a church service for them. So that morning, Dietrich Bonhoeffer, the pastor and the spy, preached his last sermon. Before he had even finished the final prayer, the door to the schoolhouse flew open. Two men with grim faces pointed and said, "Prisoner Bonhoeffer. Get ready to come with us."* Everyone in the room knew what those words meant.

Dietrich was driven north from the schoolhouse. This time Flossenbürg would be the destination. That night, he was put on trial, along with Canaris, Oster, and several others from the conspiracy. Hitler, ever acting the spiteful and petty victim, had even sent Admiral Canaris's journal down to Flossenbürg to serve as evidence in the "trial." All the conspirators were immediately found guilty and sentenced to death in the morning. Dietrich was thrown into a tiny cell alone.

HE CLOSED HIS EYES
AND LONGED FOR REST.

THAT NIGHT, HIS LAST ON THIS EARTH, DIETRICH HAD A WONDERFUL DREAM.

DIETRICH WALKED ON A GRAY AND WINDY BEACH.

HE STEPPED DOWN THROUGH A SANDY BANK, THE BROKEN SHELLS STUCK TO HIS FEET RELEASING AS THEY SANK IN THE COOL WATER. DIETRICH SHED HIS BAGS ON THE SHORE AND FELL HEADLONG INTO THE BLUE DEEP.

DOWN

HE WENT ...

EXCEPT DOWN

BECAME UP!

HE SWAM UPWARD

THROUGH THE SALTY WATER.

IT SATURATED HIS LUNGS,

BUT THE WATER FELT LIKE AIR.

THE SUN WAS DAWNING OVER THE

SURFACE ABOVE HIM. AS THE LIGHT

HIT HIS FACE, HE FELT A WEIGHT

FALL OFF HIS BODY.

LOOKING BACK, ALL HE COULD SEE WAS A SWIRLING PILLAR OF ASH AND BONES BEHIND HIM.

BUT AHEAD, THERE WAS SOMEONE STANDING ABOVE HIM, STANDING ON THE SURFACE OF THE WATER!

SUDDENLY, A STRONG HAND PLUNGED

THROUGH THE WATERY ROILING VEIL

AND HELD HIS ARM FAST.

IT JERKED, AND

DIETRICH SHUDDERED.

THE HAND LIFTED

HIM STRAIGHT UP—

INTO THE WARMTH,

INTO THE LIGHT.

"This is the end—
for me the BEGINNING
OF LIFE."*

—DIETRICH BONHOEFFER

EPILOGUE

APRIL 9, 1945 DIETRICH BONHOEFFER WAS HANGED IN A BARREN COURTYARD AT FLOSSENBÜRG CONCENTRATION CAMP. JUST TWO WEEKS LATER, THE CAMP WAS LIBERATED BY THE ADVANCING ALLIED FORCES.

DIETRICH'S BROTHER-IN-LAW HANS VON DOHNÁNYI WAS HANGED AT SACHSENHAUSEN CONCENTRATION CAMP.

APRIL 23, 1945 ON THE SAME DAY THAT FLOSSENBÜRG WAS LIBERATED, DIETRICH'S BROTHER KLAUS AND HIS BROTHER-IN-LAW RÜDIGER SCHLEICHER WERE SHOT BY A FIRING SQUAD IN THE PRISON YARD AT LEHRTER STRASSE 3, IN BERLIN.

AS THE ALLIES CLOSED IN ON BERLIN ON THE WEST, AND THE RUSSIAN ARMY MOVED IN FROM THE EAST, HITLER STILL REFUSED TO SURRENDER. FORCED TO HIDE UNDERGROUND IN HIS FÜHRERBUNKER, HITLER NEVERTHELESS COMMANDED HIS REMAINING FEW GENERALS TO PRESS THE ATTACK. BUT THE GENERALS LOOKED ON HIS COMMANDS WITH VACANT EYES AS HITLER MOVED MAKE-BELIEVE UNITS AROUND HIS WAR MAP TABLES. HITLER WAS PLAYING A BOARD GAME WITH IMAGINARY PIECES. THE NAZI INNER CIRCLE WAS TRAPPED WITH NO CHOICES BUT SURRENDER OR DEATH.

APRIL 30, 1945 ADOLF HITLER, ALONG WITH HIS MISTRESS, EVA BRAUN, KILLED THEMSELVES IN THEIR BUNKER. THEIR BODIES WERE BURNED IN A NONDESCRIPT SHELL CRATER OUTSIDE THE BUNKER.

MAY 8, 1945 THE OFFICIAL END OF WORLD WAR II IN EUROPE.

EBERHARD BETHGE, THOUGH ARRESTED BRIEFLY IN OCTOBER 1944, SURVIVED THE WAR. HE BECAME DIETRICH'S BIOGRAPHER AND THE FIRST CARETAKER OF HIS LEGACY. EBERHARD ALSO COLLECTED MUCH OF DIETRICH'S UNFINISHED WRITINGS, LETTERS, AND POEMS FROM TEGEL PRISON INTO THE BOOK "ETHICS" AND SEVERAL OTHER SIGNIFICANT VOLUMES.

MARIA SEARCHED FAITHFULLY FOR DIETRICH AFTER THE WAR ENDED. SHE TRAVELED TO THE LIBERATED CONCENTRATION CAMPS OF BUCHENWALD, DACHAU, AND FLOSSENBÜRG. IT WAS WEEKS BEFORE SHE REALIZED HE WOULD NEVER RETURN TO HER.

DIETRICH BONHOEFFER,
CIRCA 1930

AUTHOR'S NOTE

From our vantage point today, the Nazi atrocities are very easy to condemn. But how did Adolf Hitler fool a country full of so many good people? Part of my interest in telling the story of Dietrich Bonhoeffer is to offer his first-person witness to how a majestic nation can willingly become a puppet for evil. After the most casual study of the Nazi barbarity, it is easy to imagine Adolf Hitler as the worst possible leader the world will ever see, but the truth is much more frightening. Despite the lessons learned from the horrors of World War II, recent history has shown humanity has not been permanently vaccinated against tyrants. We never will be.

This story, which unfolded right in front of Dietrich, demonstrates how quickly a good and noble people can become infatuated with hatred. It is not a lesson for Germany alone. We should not see it as something that could happen only in the past. The line between national decency and a descent into fear and hatred is, and always will be, razor thin. Any nation that assumes it is too righteous to fall into these same sins will risk making the mistakes that Germany did in the 1930s.

As for the legacy of Dietrich Bonhoeffer, it is found in his unswerving belief in sacrifice on behalf of "the other." He was the polar opposite of Nazi ideology.

Dietrich was moved to take action in the face of injustice, even though he initially felt no injustice himself. This position was so radical, it eventually cost him his life. Dietrich, as a captive of the Third Reich, was executed mere weeks before its downfall. He was never truly its prisoner. Dietrich had numerous opportunities to escape his ultimate fate, but he willingly offered himself instead. For all their power and might, in the end, the Nazis could never truly conquer a heart of sacrifice.

Dietrich spent his life writing about how his belief in "the other" interacted with reality. I hope that you, the reader, can think about where you encounter "the other" in your life, and consider how you treat them. Dietrich believed that love was the same thing as sacrifice. In fact, he saw personal sacrifice as merely reflecting God's love for us—as we are His cosmic other. But it would be wrong to try to divide Dietrich's life into the sacred acts and the secular acts. If we look for a motivation for his decisions outside his furious belief in God's certainty, we will miss the very lesson he offers. Dietrich Bonhoeffer reminds us that if we hope to be a light in the world around us, we must be willing to live as unified souls.

Faith, without action, is no faith at all. Love, without sacrifice, is no love at all.

RESEARCH AND AUTHENTICITY

This story is not primarily a work of scholarship but a work of art. Though I have spent considerable time researching Dietrich Bonhoeffer, Adolf Hitler, and the Third Reich, I am not a scholar. My storytelling has relied on the hard work of those who synthesize hundreds of original sources into clear narratives. I'm extremely grateful for the invaluable work of these brilliant men and women. My retelling should not be compared with the exhaustive context of the existing biographies of Dietrich Bonhoeffer. For those interested in a more sweeping depiction of his life and work, I would highly recommend reading some of the related titles I've listed in the bibliography.

My goal was never encyclopedic detail, but underlining the essential themes found in Dietrich's life for readers. In addition, I wanted to be able to give a thumbnail account of the rise and fall of Nazi Germany. To that end, my primary decisions as an author were not what to include, but what to leave out!

FIRST EDITION OF "THE COST OF DISCIPLESHIP"

Some sections of Dietrich's life and Hitler's wartime actions have been abbreviated for clarity. (Some details I would have loved to include! One example: During his first appointment in London, Dietrich corresponded with the famous pacifist Mahatma Gandhi. Dietrich had hoped to study with him before deciding to found the Confessing Church. And there have been entire books on Hitler's peace negotiations with the British at Munich in 1938. But there isn't room for every fact, even the very notable ones!)

In the category of omissions for length: Dietrich and his fellow conspirators were not aware of the enormous scale of the Jewish Holocaust. That story of horror was not Dietrich's, so I purposely did not include extensive accounts. It would be inaccurate to use it as an emotional lever. Their work, however, was partly motivated by the heinous actions of the state against the Jewish people based on the extensive injustices they witnessed personally in Berlin.

DIETRICH'S WRITING DESK

I wish you to understand the authenticity of the dialogue and pulled quotations. It is important to know which words are authentic quotations and which are fictionalized for narrative clarity. Any text attributed to Dietrich or other characters that is marked with an asterisk is a direct quotation sourced from letters, sermons, historical documents, or personal accounts, which are given in full in the endnotes.

DIETRICH'S LAST RESIDENCE, 43 MARIENBURGER ALLEE

Otherwise, when Dietrich or other characters speak, the content should be seen as speculative. These words are used to paint a narrative picture of the time and circumstances. In some cases, there are accounts that these conversations took place, but there is not a complete record of the exact dialogue. In some passages, I speculate on Dietrich Bonhoeffer's inner state of mind, in thoughts, dreams, and prayers. These are narrative extrapolations, many of which are tonally similar to his letters, poems and journal writings. Likewise, some of the illustrations use visual metaphor and fictional staging elements. Ultimately, these devices are designed to help you on your journey with Dietrich Bonhoeffer.

ACKNOWLEDGMENTS

In the spring of 2016, I traveled to Germany in order to research and draw many of the sites mentioned in this book. I personally visited Dietrich's family home at 43 Marienburger Allee (the site where he was arrested in 1943); the church he briefly pastored in Berlin, Zionskirche; the remains of the Gestapo prison at Prinz-Albrecht-Strasse 8; and the site of his death at Flossenbürg concentration camp. To see additional sketchbook drawings from this trip, please visit www.johnhendrix.com. Thanks especially to Dr. Jutta Weber—with her assistance I had the great privilege of gaining personal access to the original papers and letters of Dietrich Bonhoeffer and Eberhard Bethge, at Staatsbibliothek zu Berlin. Huge thanks to my studio assistants, illustrator Christine Bosch and Zeke Saucedo; see more of their great work at www.christinebosch.com, and www.zekesaucedo.com. Thanks to the Sam Fox School of Design and Visual Arts, at Washington University in St. Louis, that awarded me a research grant to assist in the production of the final art for this book. Thanks to Brad Lewis and family, longtime friends and supporters of my work, who graciously helped to fund my research trip. Finally, I'm deeply grateful for the team at Abrams Books. Particularly, art director Chad W. Beckerman and my editor Howard Reeves. Howard's careful attention to the clarity, accuracy and tone of Dietrich's story has made this book immeasurably better than I ever could have produced without him.

SELECTED BIBLIOGRAPHY

ARCHIVAL SOURCES

Papers of Dietrich Bonhoeffer and Papers of Eberhard Bethge, Staatsbibliothek zu Berlin.

LITERATURE

Alexander, Bevin. *Inside the Nazi War Machine: How Three Generals Unleashed Hitler's Blitzkrieg upon the World.* New York: Penguin/NAL Caliber, 2010.

Basset, Richard. *Hitler's Spy Chief, The Wilhelm Canaris Betrayal.* New York: Pegasus, 2012.

Beevor, Antony. *The Fall of Berlin, 1945.* New York: Viking, 2002.

Bethge, Eberhard. *Dietrich Bonhoeffer: A Biography.* Ed. Victoria J. Barnett, trans. Eric Mosbacher et al. Minneapolis, MN: Augsburg Fortress Press, 2000.

———, Renate Bethge, and Christian Gremmels. *Dietrich Bonhoeffer: A Life in Pictures.* Philadelphia: Fortress Press, 1986.

Boeselager, Philipp Freiherr von. *Valkyrie: The Story of the Plot to Kill Hitler, by Its Last Member.* With Florence and Jerome Fehrenbach, trans. Steven Rendall. New York: Vintage Books, 2009.

Bonhoeffer, Dietrich. *Christ the Center.* Trans. Edwin Robertson. New York: Harper & Row, 1978.

———. *The Cost of Discipleship.* New York: SCM Press Limited/Touchstone, 1959.

———. *Ethics.* Ed. Eberhard Bethge, trans. Neville Horton Smith. New York: Macmillan, 1955.

———. *Letters & Papers from Prison.* Enlarged Edition, Ed. Eberhard Bethge, trans. Reginald H. Fuller. New York: SCM Press Limited/Touchstone, 1971.

———. *Life Together.* Trans. John W. Doberstein. New York: Harper & Row, 1954.

———, and Maria von Wedemeyer. *Love Letters from Cell 92: The Correspondence between Dietrich Bonhoeffer and Maria von Wedemeyer, 1943–1945.* Ed. Ruth-Alice von Bismarck and Ulrich Kabitz, trans. John Brown. Nashville: Abingdon Press, 1995.

Giblin, James Cross. *The Life and Death of Adolf Hitler.* New York: Clarion Books, 2002.

Goddard, Donald. *The Last Days of Dietrich Bonhoeffer.* New York: Harper & Row, 1976.

Hoyt, Edwin P. *Hitler's War.* New York: McGraw-Hill, 1988.

Hitler, Adolf. *Mein Kampf.* Trans. Ralph Manheim. Boston: Houghton Mifflin, 1971.

Jordan, David, and Andrew Wiest. *Atlas of World War II: Over 160 Detailed Battle & Campaign Maps.* New York: Barnes & Noble Books. 2004.

Larson, Erik. *In the Garden of Beasts: Love, Terror, and an American Family in Hitler's Berlin.* New York: Broadway Books, 2012.

March, Charles. *Strange Glory: A Life of Dietrich Bonhoeffer.* New York: Alfred A. Knopf, 2014.

Metaxas, Eric. *Bonhoeffer: Pastor, Martyr, Prophet, Spy: A Righteous Gentile vs. the Third Reich.* Nashville: Thomas Nelson, 2010.

Shirer, William L. *The Rise and Fall of the Third Reich: A History of Nazi Germany.* New York: Simon & Schuster, 2011.

Van Dyke, Michael. *The Story of Dietrich Bonhoeffer: Radical Integrity.* Uhrichville, OH: Barbour Publishing, 2001.

Zimmerman, Wolf-Dieter. *I Knew Dietrich Bonhoeffer.* New York: Harper & Row, 1966.

NOTES

EPIGRAPH

Pages 1–2: "This is the end—for me the beginning of life." Bethge, *Dietrich Bonhoeffer*, p. 927.

1 THE YOUNG THEOLOGIAN

PAGE 8: "Does the good God love . . ." Metaxas, *Bonhoeffer*, p. 11.

PAGE 12: "In that case, I shall reform it!" Bethge, *Dietrich Bonhoeffer*, p. 36.

PAGE 15: German inflation, Hoyt, *Hitler's War*, p. 5.

PAGE 18: "I had at last come . . ." Adolf Hitler, *Mein Kampf*, p. 61.

PAGE 18: "poisoners are . . ." Ibid, p. 338.

PAGE 18: "The personification . . ." Ibid., p. 324.

2 A YOUNG GERMAN IN HARLEM

PAGE 32: "The separation of whites . . ." Marsh, *Strange Glory*, p. 114.

PAGE 32: "the conditions are . . ." Metaxas, *Bonhoeffer*, p. 109.

PAGE 32: "The way the southerners talk . . ." Marsh, *Strange Glory*, p. 133.

PAGE 37: "The church is the church only . . . " Bonhoeffer, *Letters & Papers from Prison*, pp. 382-383.

3 GOD IS MY FÜHRER

PAGE 48: "When a leader allows . . ." Van Dyke, *The Story of Dietrich Bonhoeffer*, p. 59.

PAGE 48: "Leaders or offices which . . ." Metaxas, *Bonhoeffer*, p. 142.

PAGE 52: "continually ask the state . . ." Ibid, p. 153.

PAGE 52: "The Jewish question troubles . . ." Bethge, *Dietrich Bonhoeffer*, pp. 271–272.

PAGE 52: "It is not enough . . ." Dietrich Bonhoeffer, "The Church and the Jewish Question" in *No Rusty Swords: Letters, Lectures and Notes* 1928–1936 (New York: Harper & Row, 1965), p. 227.

PAGE 53: "If you board the wrong train . . ." Zimmerman, *I Knew Dietrich Bonhoeffer*, p. 129.

PAGE 55: "To delay or fail to make a decision . . ." Dietrich Bonhoeffer, *London, 1933–1935: Dietrich Bonhoeffer*, ed. Keith Clements, trans. Isabel Best (Minneapolis: Fortress Press, 2007), pp. 126–127.

4 THE DECISION

PAGE 66: "After the end of the Olympiade . . ." Bethge, *Dietrich Bonhoeffer*, p. 536.

PAGE 69: "First they came for the socialists . . ." Metaxas, *Bonhoeffer*, p. 192.

PAGE 77: "They burned all the meeting-places . . ." Marsh, *Strange Glory*, p. 272.

PAGE 84: "All I need is Germany . . ." Ibid., p. 280.

PAGE 85: "I know which of these alternatives . . ." Ibid., p. 284.

5 JAMMING THE SPOKE

PAGE 91: "Who stands fast? . . ." Bonhoeffer, *Letters & Papers from Prison*, p. 5.

PAGE 92: "If I saw a lunatic plowing his car . . ." Marsh, *Strange Glory*, p. 346.

PAGE 104: "We shall have to run risks . . ." Bethge, *Dietrich Bonhoeffer*, p. 681.

PAGE 108: "If you want to know the truth . . ." Metaxas, *Bonhoeffer*, p. 387.

NOTES (CONTINUED)

PAGE 114: "I want to care for you . . ." Dietrich Bonhoeffer, *Conspiracy and Imprisonment, 1940–1945*, ed. Mark S. Brocker, trans. Lisa E. Dahill with Douglas W. Stott (Minneapolis, MN: Fortress Press, 2006), pp. 383–384.

PAGE 115: "We must prove . . ." Shirer, *The Rise and Fall of the Third Reich*, p. 1043.

6 THE PASTOR IN BLOCK 92

PAGE 127: "Be strong. Admit nothing." Marsh, *Strange Glory*, p. 359.

PAGE 129: " . . . the wind sometimes bears . . ." Bonhoeffer, *Letters & Papers from Prison*, p. 119.

PAGE 129: "It makes me furious . . ." Ibid., p. 136.

PAGE 130: "I-M N-O-T C-E-R-T-A-I-N . . ." Metaxas, *Bonhoeffer*, p. 443.

PAGE 131: "Like a polar bear." Bonhoeffer, *Letters & Papers from Prison*, p. 39.

PAGE 133: "Joy is a thing that we want . . ." Ibid., p. 49.

PAGE 136: "Some cruel fellow went and destroyed the lot . . ." Ibid., p. 71.

PAGE 137: "A great deal here is horrible, but where isn't it?" Ibid., p. 232.

PAGE 138: "My grim experiences often pursue me . . ." Ibid., p. 162.

PAGE 139: "In my experience, nothing tortures us more . . ." Ibid., p. 167.

PAGE 144: "Red paper and stain on mug . . ." Marsh, *Strange Glory*, p. 359.

PAGE 145: "It's time now for something to be done . . ." Joachim Fest, *Plotting Hitler's Death: The Story of the German Resistance* (New York: Metropolitan Books, 1996), pp. 240–241.

PAGE 150: "Fate has offered us this opportunity . . ." Metaxas, *Bonhoeffer*, p. 479.

PAGE 151: "Long live our . . ." Shirer, *The Rise and Fall of the Third Reich*, p. 1068.

7 THE END, THE BEGINNING

PAGE 157: "The ultimate question . . ." Bonhoeffer, *Letters & Papers from Prison*, p. 7.

PAGE 158: "He was determined to resist . . ." Zimmerman, *I Knew Dietrich Bonhoeffer*, p. 226.

PAGE 158: "If we want to be Christians . . ." Bonhoeffer, *Letters & Papers from Prison*, p. 14.

PAGE 159: "Suffer faithfully," Bonhoeffer, *London, 1933–1935: Dietrich Bonhoeffer*, ed. Keith Clements, trans. Isabel Best (Minneapolis: Fortress Press, 2007), p 196.

PAGE 159: "I do not think that death . . ." Bonhoeffer, *Letters & Papers from Prison*, p. 16.

PAGE 159: " . . . words from the Bible." Ibid., p. 419.

PAGE 163: "Prisoner Bonhoeffer. Get ready . . ." S. Payne Best, *The Venlo Incident,* (Waterford, England: Hutchinson, 1950), p. 200.

PAGE 167: "This is the end—for me the beginning of life." Bethge, *Dietrich Bonhoeffer*, p. 927.

ENDPAPERS

PAGE 176: "We have been silent witnesses . . ." Bonhoeffer, *Letters & Papers from Prison*, p. 16.

KZ FLOSSENBÜRG,

INDEX

"WE HAVE BEEN SILENT WITNESSES OF EVIL DEEDS; WE HAVE
BEEN DRENCHED BY MANY STORMS; WE HAVE LEARNT THE ARTS
OF EQUIVOCATION AND PRETENSE; EXPERIENCE HAS MADE
US SUSPICIOUS OF OTHERS AND KEPT US FROM BEING TRUTHFUL
AND OPEN; INTOLERABLE CONFLICTS HAVE WORN US DOWN AND
EVEN MADE US CYNICAL. ARE WE STILL OF ANY USE?"*

—DIETRICH BONHOEFFER, JANUARY 1943

To Holly, my sister, my first friend.
To Rebecca Sherman, for steadfast belief in this book from the beginning.

The illustrations in this book were created with hand drawn pencil and custom digital brushes created for this
project by Kyle T. Webster. The images were colored digitally on a Wacom Cintiq drawing tablet. The text is
set in a custom typeface based on my handwriting, built by John Martz. The book is printed in black,
Pantone 3262U, and Pantone Red 032U spot colors.

Library of Congress Cataloging-in-Publication Data
Names: Hendrix, John, 1976- author.
Title: The faithful spy : Dietrich Bonhoeffer and the plot to kill Hitler / by John Hendrix.
Description: New York : Amulet Books, 2018.
Identifiers: LCCN 2017032171 | ISBN 978-1-4197-2838-9 (hardcover, jacketed, picture)
Subjects: LCSH: Bonhoeffer, Dietrich, 1906–1945—Juvenile literature. |
Hitler, Adolf, 1889–1945—Assassination attempts—Juvenile literature. |
Anti-Nazi movement—Germany—Biography—Juvenile literature. |
Government, Resistance to—Germany—History—20th century—Juvenile literature. |
Church and state—Germany—History—20th century—Juvenile literature. |
Theologians—Germany—Biography—Juvenile literature.
Classification: LCC BX4827.B57 H454 2018 | DDC 230/.044092 [B]—dc23

ISBN for paperback 978-1-4197-3265-2

Text copyright and illustrations copyright © 2018 John Hendrix
Photo credit page 168: pbk Bildagentur / Art Resource NY
Book design by John Hendrix

ABRAMS The Art of Books
195 Broadway, New York, NY 10007
abramsbooks.com